THE SPIRIT OF THE
OXFORD MOVEMENT

THE SPIRIT OF THE OXFORD MOVEMENT

By

CHRISTOPHER DAWSON

LONDON
SHEED & WARD
MCMXXXIII

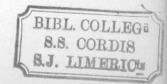

PRINTED IN GREAT BRITAIN
BY THE WHITEFRIARS PRESS LTD.
LONDON AND TONBRIDGE
FOR SHEED AND WARD
31 PATERNOSTER ROW,
LONDON, E.C.4
AND 63 FIFTH AVENUE,
NEW YORK
FIRST PUBLISHED SEPTEMBER 1933

PREFACE

It may be thought that some apology is needed for adding to the already copious supply of literature that has been called forth by the centenary of the Oxford Movement. The greater part of that literature is, however, written by and for those to whom the Oxford Movement is a household word, and it has been their object to commemorate its achievements in a spirit of filial piety rather than to explain its significance. There is still plenty of room for the work of historical interpretation. Few things are more difficult to understand than the mind of the immediate past, and the difficulty is greatest at the interval of a century—an interval which is too long to be bridged by living memory, but too short to stimulate the exercise of the historical imagination. It seems familiar ground, yet as soon as we enter upon it we find ourselves in a strange country, among men who speak a different language from ourselves. As the age of Wordsworth could not appreciate the age of Pope, and the age of Pope could not understand the age of Donne, so it is with the present age and the age of the Oxford Movement. We have a different scale of values and different intellectual interests, and the motives and ideals which were accepted as unquestionable by the men of the Oxford Movement appear to us in the last degree forced and unnatural. This is to be seen most clearly in Mr.

Geoffrey Faber's book, *Oxford Apostles*, which is almost
the only serious attempt to interpret the Oxford
Movement to the present age in an entirely independent
fashion without appealing to the traditional judgements
of ecclesiastical historians. He bases his history of the
Movement on his interpretation of the character of its
leaders and he bases this interpretation not on their
own theological and moral conceptions but on the
categories of modern psychology. The result of this
psychological analysis of the Oxford Movement is to
produce a strange reversal of the traditional values.
Seen through Freudian spectacles the severe moralism
of the Tractarian ethos dissolved into an orgy of
morbid emotionalism. The history of the Oxford
Movement becomes an essay in sexual psychopathy.
Newman appears not as one of the greatest of English
religious thinkers but as an example of the unfortunate
results of infantile repression, and his spiritual development is not the result of his religious principles ; on
the contrary the latter are the unconscious instruments
of a maimed personality struggling to attain equilibrium
without abandoning " the citadel where his infantile
self lay entrenched." In the same way Froude and
Pusey represent different types of psychic perversion
while the smaller fry are summarily dismissed as
Newman's " escort of hermaphrodites."

Mr. Faber recognizes that the conclusions which
psychologists have drawn from the study of subnormal
patients cannot be applied without qualification to the
personality of a genius such as Newman. But since the
importance of the Oxford Movement is entirely
dependent on its spiritual achievement we may well

ask what help we are likely to get from a method which explains personality by reducing human behaviour to its physical and non-rational elements.

A psychology which ignores religious values must inevitably misinterpret the behaviour of men whose whole lives are ruled by religious motives. This is particularly evident in Mr. Faber's treatment of Hurrell Froude. The intimacy of the latter's self-revelation seems at first sight ideal material for psychological analysis, but actually it is full of pitfalls. In the case of the ordinary man repression may well point to the existence of some morbid psychic complex, but with a man like Froude who exercises a deliberate and conscious repression over all his natural instincts, however apparently innocent they may be, the situation is different. The unwary Freudian who regards Froude's anguished self-accusation as evidence of some typical perversion may be disconcerted to find that he is dealing not with some dark hidden sensuality but with an unmortified desire for roast goose or with a secret brooding over the pleasure of a day's yachting.[1] " I am

---

[1] This is certainly the case with the passage in the Journal which is the mainstay of Mr. Faber's theory on Froude's homosexuality. Froude's self-accusation with regard to his first undergraduate pupil has nothing to do with any guilty passion ; it is simply due to his characteristic dread of making the attempt to do good to others an excuse for self-assertion and self-satisfaction. Mr. Faber's other proof of his thesis from Froude's poem on " The Old and New Self " is even weaker and is a typical example of the dangers of the Freudian exegesis. Froude concludes his verses with a well-known tag from the seventh Eclogue

Haec memini et victum frustra contendere Thyrsin
Ex illo Corydon Corydon est tempore nobis.

Froude's intention is, obviously, to emphasize the victory of the new self —Corydon—over the old self—Thyrsis—who continues to strive in defeat. Mr. Faber, however, argues that since the new self is the last speaker in Froude's poem and Thyrsis is the last speaker in the Eclogue,

becoming careless and sensual," he writes in his journal, " I often arise from my meals conscious that I have eaten more than I ought. . . . And in my prayers my thoughts run off on boats or some romance of the sort. . . . And often when I have fancied I am disgusted with myself for indulging too much at dinner I fail to infer from it that I must eat less at tea " (*Remains* I., p. 451).

In the same way, Mr. Faber's ignorance of the religious language of the period leads him to misunderstand a passage in Newman's letters dealing with his relations with Froude, " I have thought," wrote Newman, " vows (of celibacy) are evidence of *want of faith* (*i.e.*, trust)." Mr. Faber supposes that Froude had proposed a mutual pledge of celibacy and that Newman objected to this as suggesting want of faith *in one another*. Actually, however, Newman means that the making of a formal vow shows want of trust *in God* and he makes this quite clear by the words that follow : " Why should we look to the morrow ? It will be given us to do our duty as the day comes ; to bind duty by forestalment is to lay up manna for seven days ; it will corrupt us."

Such mistakes are the nemesis of a psychology which regards every spiritual or self-transcending tendency as a disguised form of the sexual impulse. But this is not its only disadvantage. Even more serious is the confusion of moral and medical values which is the besetting sin of the literary psychologist. The Freu-

therefore Corydon is the old self and it is the latter which is victorious. But this is not all ; in the *second* Eclogue Corydon is the lover of the fair Alexis, *therefore* Froude intends to confess the " vile affections " of his old self. Q.E.D. Comment is needless !

dian method in itself is entirely indifferent to moral considerations, but as soon as it is transferred from the consulting room of the psychiatrist to the use of the historian and the man of letters, it becomes contaminated with the moral convictions and prejudices of the lay critic.

Thus the Freudian concept of homosexuality involves no moral judgement, but as applied by Mr. Faber to the case of Newman it becomes charged with ethical significance and finally becomes equivalent to a lack of " manliness " in the moral sense. This is, however, nothing else but the old prejudices of Kingsley and Abbott in a new Freudian dress. No doubt there is much to be said for the traditional English ideal of manliness which finds expression in Mr. Kipling's " If." But it was not Newman's ideal, and we have no right to ignore his own ethical standards and to judge his character by a conflation of the Freudian psychology with the ethical ideals of Mr. Rudyard Kipling.

The fact is that Newman offends the moral sense of his critics not because he was weak but because he was strong. His genius challenges the accepted standards of the ordinary Englishman who is accustomed to dismiss the great ethical paradoxes of Christianity as pious platitudes. The essential principles of Newman's ethic are far from being peculiar to him alone. They are common to the whole Oxford Movement : indeed they form part of the common inheritance of Christianity. But the imaginative power and intellectual subtlety of Newman's mind revealed them with a clarity which startled the utilitarian optimism of

Victorian culture and the sentimental humanitarianism of modern religion. When we read the criticisms of Kingsley or Abbott, it is, at first sight, surprising to find that their most frenzied denunciations are directed not so much against Newman's sacerdotalism or sacramentalism as against his reassertion of the fundamental principles of Pauline and Augustinian theology—the transcendence of the supernatural order and the incommensurability of Nature and Grace. Thus the passage which shocked Kingsley so much, in which Newman asserts the spiritual superiority of a dirty and untruthful beggar woman who lives a religious life over " the State's pattern man " who possesses all the civic virtues but is lacking in faith, hope and charity,[1] is the merest commonplace of Christian ethics, and the only thing that renders it shocking is that Newman had made it seem real. In the same way Dr. Abbott is willing to accept the New Testament opposition between the Church and the world as having some justification in the age of Nero, but he is horrified at Newman's conviction that it still retains its meaning for the age of Victoria.[2]

It was this determination to realize the primitive " apostolic " conception of Christianity and to apply it uncompromisingly to modern conditions that was at

[1] " What then does Dr. Newman Mean " in W. Ward's ed. of the *Apologia* (Oxford, 1913) pp. 47-48. It is characteristic of Kingsley's fantastic reasoning that he condemns this characteristically Augustinian point of view as Pelagian and then goes on to make it responsible for the debased state of the Celtic Irish population, since it tends to make them look down on the Protestant gentry " who try to introduce among them capital, industry, civilization, and above all, that habit of speaking the truth, for want of which they are what they are, and are likely to remain such as long as they have Dr. Newman for their teacher ! "

[2] *The Anglican Career of Cardinal Newman*, I., pp. 15-16, II., p. 12.

once the great strength of the Oxford Movement and
the great obstacle to its acceptance. It brought the
Movement into conscious conflict with the spirit of
the age—with the utilitarianism and secularism of
19th century Liberalism, and with the rationalism and
naturalism of modern thought. This has undoubtedly
had a prejudicial influence on the reputation of the
Oxford Movement, since it has made it easy for its
opponents to identify it with the cause of reaction and
obscurantism. We must, however, remember that
Liberalism and Rationalism are by no means identical
with the principles of Reason and Liberty. In the
religious sphere, which was its proper territory, the
Oxford Movement stood for spiritual freedom against
Erastianism and for a scientific theology against the
emotional religiosity of popular Protestantism. Even
in the secular sphere, the anti-Liberalism of the Oxford
Movement is not a proof of its insensitiveness to the
need for social reform. On the contrary, its hostility to
Liberalism was due, at least in part, to its dissatisfaction
with a social system which seemed dedicated to the
service of Mammon. In so far as the Oxford Movement
was Tory, its Toryism was not that of the defenders of
vested interests, the " Conservatives " who aroused
Hurrell Froude's scorn, but that of Southey and
Coleridge and the young Disraeli who were among the
first to denounce the injustices of the Industrial Revolution and the new Poor Law, and the evils of the factory
systems.[1]

[1] Cf. especially Southey's dialogues on society, *Sir Thomas More*
(1829), which show the general attitude to social questions of the anti-
Liberal traditionalists of the period.

In the same way the anti-Rationalism of the leaders of the Oxford Movement does not prove that they undervalued reason or the things of the mind. They were opposed to the spirit of rationalism in religion just because they were intelligent enough to realize its intellectual inadequacy. To eliminate the element of mystery from religion, to measure the transcendant and the eternal by finite and temporal standards is not to make religion rational, but to misconceive its real nature and thereby to impoverish the human mind and to narrow its range of vision.

Newman, on the other hand, used his reason in matters of religion so as to enlarge the frontiers of spiritual consciousness and to open the shuttered windows of the human mind to the vast spiritual horizon that lay around it.

In this and in other respects the Oxford Movement was a protest against the limitations of its own age and culture, and the very fact that it was a minority movement in opposition to the victorious spirit of the age should perhaps make it more comprehensible to an age which is itself intensely critical of the dominant features of 19th century culture. As Kierkegaard has come into his own, on the Continent, now that the tide of Liberal Protestantism has ebbed, so should it be with Newman and the Oxford Movement in this country. And this might be so, were it not for the difficulty of bridging the intellectual gulf that lies between us. The educated man of to-day no longer understands the highly specialized theological tradition of the past. Theology is no longer a part of English education and consequently Newman and Pusey and

Keble speak to us in a dead language.   It is for this reason that I have quoted so largely from the verses of *Lyra Apostolica*.   The language of poetry, even though it be minor poetry, is more universal than the language of theological controversy, and the *Lyra* expresses the spirit of the Oxford Movement even more clearly and directly than the *Tracts for the Times* themselves.   It is the purpose of the following essay to do something to bridge this gulf and to attempt to explain the intellectual traditions and the social environment from which the Oxford Movement sprang.   It is not enough to study the characters of the men who made it, or rather it is only possible to understand their characters by understanding the spiritual world in which they lived, the ideas that moved them and the faith that inspired their action.

I wish to express my thanks to Messrs. Longmans, Green & Co. for permission to quote from the *Letters and Correspondence of John Henry Newman* edited by Anne Mozley, 1891.

CONTENTS

THE SPIRIT OF THE OXFORD MOVEMENT

I. *THE ANGLICAN TRADITION*

THE ONE WAY

One only Way to Life ;
One Faith, delivered once for all ;
One holy Band, endowed with Heaven's high call ;
One earnest, endless Strife ;—
This is the Church th' Eternal framed of old.

Smooth open ways, good store ;
A Creed for every clime and age,
By Mammon's touch new moulded o'er and o'er ;
No cross, no war to wage ;—
This is the Church our earth-dimmed eyes behold.

But ways must have an end,
Creeds undergo the trial flame,
Nor with th' impure the Saints for ever blend,
Heaven's glory with our shame :
Think on that hour, and choose 'twixt soft and bold.

JOHN KEBLE.

THE centenary of the Oxford Movement has already produced no small amount of literature in which almost every aspect of that movement has been exhaustively discussed. With few exceptions, however, these commemorative essays are concerned with the Oxford Movement only in so far as it was the source and origin of the Anglo-Catholic development in the Church of England. They are panegyrics or criticisms of a living ecclesiastical movement. They discuss the past with their eye upon the present, and they are often more concerned to justify present ideals by precedents of the past than to discover those elements in the past that are most peculiarly its own, and from which it derives its characteristic uniqueness.

It is always a temptation to the historian to exaggerate the continuity of history, above all when the historian is the representative of a party or a cause. But the past does not exist for the sake of the present, it has its own ends and its own values. Its life is bound up with the life of unique individual personalities, which may seem to be mere fodder for the historical process but which are nevertheless spiritual ultimates ; that is the profound mystery of history which Newman has expressed so nobly in the lines which he wrote in 1833 during his voyage in the Ionian Sea :—

> That multitudinous stream we now note down,
> As though one life, in birth and in decay.
> Yet, is their being's history spent and run
> Whose spirits live in awful singleness
> Each in his self-formed sphere of light or gloom ? [1]

Thus history is not unlike Dante's journey through the other world. If we enter deeply into a spiritual epoch like that of the Oxford Movement, we find ourselves in the presence of men whose spirits still live and have power to move us. For the men who count in the end are not the successful men who rode triumphantly on the crest of the wave of change, like Napoleon, but those who are indifferent to success or failure, who despise quick results and preserve their spiritual integrity at all costs. It is they who are the real judges of the world. *Fulgebunt justi et tamquam scintillæ in arundineto discurrent. Judicabunt nationes et*

[1] *Corcyra* in *Lyra Apostolica*, XLVIII.

dominabuntur populis et regnabit Dominus illorum in perpetuum.

But apart from these deeper considerations, the Oxford Movement deserves to be studied for its own sake, and not merely for its effects on the subsequent fortunes of the Church of England. It is a very original and characteristic phase of the English tradition, for it represents that unique moment in the history of our culture when English society had emerged from the stability of the Georgian world and had not yet become set in the mould of Victorianism. That comparatively short period witnessed an extraordinary flowering of the national genius such as England had not known since the Elizabethan age. Like the latter, it was an age of poets and soldiers, of men of thought and men of action. The English mind was more adventurous, more alive to ideas, less stodgy and provincial than either before or since. It is true that it was an age of crisis and widespread distress, when England was already overshadowed by the lowering cloud of an industrialism that was beginning to pollute the English air and to deface the English countryside. It shared some of the worst faults of the two ages between which it stood—the animal brutality of the past and the mechanical hardness of the future, but it also contained seeds of promise that the future was not to fulfil and the last fruits of the old order that passed away with it. Such was the Oxford Movement. It was the last fruit of the old Anglican tradition that had its roots in the 17th century, and at the same time it brought the English tradition out of its spiritual isolation into contact with the main currents of western culture, with Catholicism and Liberalism. Hitherto the English attitude to the world outside had been one of jealous exclusivism. The French Revolution had produced a national reaction against " Jacobin " ideas and had made a devotion to " Church and King " the standard of patriotism, while for more than two centuries the whole national tradition had been bound with a fanatical hatred of foreign Popery, of everything Popish because it was foreign and of everything foreign because it was Popish. There is a delightful story of how during the French wars of the early 18th century an ape, that had escaped from a travelling show, was arrested by a zealous constable as a French spy, and this attitude to the foreigner still survived in the England of the Reform Bill. Gladstone has related how in his first experience of English politics, at the great Reform election of 1831, he was struck by two things, the universal hostility of the ordinary voter to Catholic emancipation, and his contemptuous indifference to Continental politics. " I held forth," he writes, " to a working man on the established text 'Reform was revolution.' To corroborate my doctrine, I said, ' Why, look at the revolutions in foreign coun-tries,' meaning, of course, France and Belgium. The man looked hard at me and said these words : ' Damn all foreign countries, what has old England to do with foreign countries ? ' " [1]

But in spite of the strength of this tradition, it was no longer possible for England to stand aside and take no part in the world's debate. Behind the party

[1] Morley's *Life of Gladstone*, I, 54 (ed. 1908).

of Reform stood Bentham and the Utilitarians, and behind them again the philosophy of the French Enlightenment and its rationalist idealism. Behind the Tories, on the other hand, stood Coleridge, and behind him the German philosophy of the Romantic age with its religious idealism and its cult of historical development and its admiration for mediæval Christendom. The passing of the Reform Bill brought these forces into direct conflict. But it was not the reform of the State but that of the Church which proved to be the decisive issue. It was this question, as John Morley has written, that " opened the sluices and let out the flood. What is the Church of England ? To ask that question was to ask a hundred others. Creeds, dogmas, ordinances, hierarchy, parliamentary institutions, judicial tribunals, historical tradition—the prayer-book, the Bible—all these enormous topics, sacred and profane, with all their countless ramifications were rapidly swept into a tornado of such controversy as had not been seen in England since the Revolution." [1]

At first sight the cause of all this seems very disproportionate to the effects, and there is something incongruous in the spectacle of an unworldly idealist like Keble announcing the hour of national apostasy because the State had taken in hand the reform of the Irish State Church, which was not even the Church of the nation, and which owed not only its wealth but its very existence to an alien secular power.

Nevertheless the moderate and reasonable measures of ecclesiastical reform, that were actually passed by

[1] *Ibid.*, I, 116.

the new Government, formed part of a wider programme which really did involve a change in the fundamental relations between Church and State in England, and the new Erastianism of Lord Brougham and Lord John Russell bore a very different character from that of the Tudors or the Stuarts. The old Church of England was a national Church in the very fullest sense of the word. Its relation to the State was not a matter of external policy and organization, it was an almost sacramental bond which moulded the inner life and spiritual ethos of the community. The Anglican tradition asserted the sacred character of kingship in the most unequivocal terms, and it rejected the idea of any limitation of the royal authority to purely temporal matters as " a very wicked and brutish opinion," as though, in Hooker's words, " God had ordained kings for no other end and purpose but only to fat up men like hogs and to see that they have their mast." [1]

In the great age of the Church of England these ideas found characteristic expression in the doctrines of the Divine Right of Kings and the duty of Passive Obedience, and though they suffered a serious reverse owing to the Revolution of 1688 and the schism of the Non-jurors, it would be a mistake to suppose that they were no longer current in the 18th and early 19th centuries.

They were upheld not only by the extreme High Churchmen who characteristically made the doctrine of Passive Obedience an instrument of resistance to the Government, but they were equally characteristic of

[1] *Eccles. Polity*, VIII, iii ,2.

Whigs such as Archbishop Gibson and Dr. Routh,[1] the last representative of the old order in a changed world, who in spite of their adhesion to the Revolution Settlement and their rejection of Passive Obedience were as firm as Laud or Sancroft in their devotion to the High Church tradition. Moreover, the renewal of the alliance between the monarchy and the Tories which marked the age of George III. had restored the influence of the High Church party in the Establishment, and for nearly seventy years they had enjoyed a practical monopoly of government patronage, while their ideal of the union of Church and State had received a powerful reinforcement from the teaching of political philosophers and men of letters, like Burke and Coleridge and Southey. And these ideas were not merely the badge of a political party or an ecclesiastical faction, they possessed the highest possible sanction in the liturgy of the Church itself. All through the age of the Revolution and the Whig supremacy, and until long after the Reform Bill itself, the Church of England had kept the State festivals which commemorate the Gunpowder Treason, the Execution of King Charles the Martyr, and the Restoration of the Royal Family. If we wish to understand the ethos of the old Church of England, which united religion and politics in a common loyalty, we cannot do better than read the liturgical offices for these days as well as the sermons which accompanied them, as, for example, the sermon of Isaac Barrow for May 29, 1676, on the King's Happy

[1] Dr. Routh's Whiggism is vouched for by William Palmer in his *Notes of a Visit to the Russian Church*, pp. 8-9 (1882).

Return, that of Sacheverel on Nov. 5, 1709, on Perils among False Brethren, that of Bishop Horsley on King Charles' Day, 1793, that of Keble for King Charles' Day, 1831, on the Danger of Sympathizing with Rebellion, and that of Pusey for Nov. 5, 1837, on Passive Obedience.[1]

This is not mere Erastianism in the vulgar sense, it inspired a genuine warmth of religious feeling, and it was associated with all that was best in the Church of England and much that was finest in the national tradition. It is the spirit of Hooker and Andrewes, and Laud and Sancroft and Henry Vaughan and Thomas Ken. The perfume that still clings to the little church of Bemerton and the chapel of Little Gidding, to Coleshill and Shottesbrook and King's Cliffe, is the perfume of a double loyalty. It was in this atmosphere that the progenitors of the Oxford Movement were bred. This was fully recognized by the opponents of the movement as by Thomas Arnold, in

---

[1] *E.g.*, the concluding collect of the service for May 29.

" Almighty God, our heavenly Father, who of Thine infinite and unspeakable goodness towards us didst in a most extraordinary and wonderful manner disappoint and overthrow the wicked designs of those traiterous, heady, and high minded men, who under the pretence of Religion and Thy most holy name, had contrived and well-nigh effected the utter destruction of this Church and Kingdom : As we do this day most heartily and devoutly adore and magnify Thy glorious name, for this thine infinite goodness already vouchsafed to us ; so do we most humbly beseech Thee to continue Thy grace and favour towards us, that no such dismal calamity may ever again fall upon us. Infatuate and defeat all the secret counsels of deceitful and wicked men against us ; Abate their pride, assuage their malice and confound their devices. Strengthen the hands of our gracious Sovereign King George, and all that are put in authority under him, with judgement and justice, to cut off all such workers of iniquity, as turn Religion into Rebellion, and Faith into Faction ; that they may never again prevail against us nor triumph in the ruin of the Monarchy and Thy Church among us."

1836, when he wrote : " They are the very Non-jurors and High Church clergy of King William's and Anne's and George the First's time reproduced with scarcely a shade of difference."

No doubt the average High Churchman only accepted this tradition in its cruder and more Erastian form, like Archdeacon Froude who, in his son James Anthony's words, regarded " the Church itself as part of the Constitution, and the Prayer Book as an act of Parliament which only folly or disloyalty could quarrel with." Nevertheless, it was implicit in the High Church tradition, and it is difficult to draw any strict line of demarcation between High Churchmen like Sykes and Watson and Keble and Rose, who preserved the genuine 17th century tradition, and men like Dr. Hook and Christopher Wordsworth, the younger, who represent the more official type. The same theological traditions and the same type of piety were common to both schools, the differences were differences of degree rather than of principle, and the views which Dr. Hook championed so warmly in his famous sermon before Queen Victoria in 1838 are the same as those which inspired Keble's assize sermon of 1833.

To the supporters of this tradition the new movement of reform awakened memories of the past and seemed to portend a new attack on the rights and liberties of the Established Church like that of the Cromwellian Age. Almost to a man the High Churchmen were High Tories, the diehards of the hopeless resistance to Catholic Emancipation and to the Reform Bill. But it was difficult to maintain the old loyalties in the new world. If Lord Brougham was no Cromwell,

William IV was an even less satisfactory substitute for Charles I. All the traditional allies of the High Church, the Crown, the Bishops, the Tory Ministry, proved broken reeds. The Reform Bill had destroyed the bases of the old alliance. Henceforward the High Church was to stand more and more for ecclesiastical autonomy and independence of the State. The true heirs of the Tudor settlement were to be the Broad Churchmen, the followers of Arnold and Stanley, who pursued the latitudinarian ideal of comprehensiveness rather than Catholicism, and who were prepared to make almost any sacrifice to preserve the national character of the Established Church.

It is true that the classical Anglican theory of Church and State still found champions in early Victorian times, notably in the young Gladstone and in Christopher Wordsworth junior,[1] but their paper ideals were easily vanquished by the hard common sense of a Liberal journalist of genius like Macaulay.[2] This, however, was not the path which the Oxford Movement was destined to follow. Its direction was determined by men who accepted the breakdown of the old alliance and the passing of the old order. Their ideal was not the Tudor Settlement, nor the Church State of Hooker, nor even the quasi-Byzantine theocracy of Laud and Strafford : it was the spiritual freedom of the Apostolic Church and the Catholic inheritance of the Church of the Fathers. The assertion of this ideal was due above all to the genius of the youngest and most

[1] W. G. Gladstone, *The State in Its Relations with the Church*, 1838 ; and Christopher Wordsworth, *Theophilus Anglicanus*, 1843.
[2] In his famous article on Gladstone's book in *The Edinburgh Review*, April, 1839.

brilliant of the Oxford group, Richard Hurrell Froude, who from his death bed aimed the arrows of his wit and scorn at the Erastian compromise and the Reformation settlement itself—an arch Tory who was the sworn foe of Conservatism, a High Churchman who loathed the worldliness and fat complacency of the official High Church party. It is in the action of this man on the two highly dissimilar and original characters of Keble and Newman that the true genesis of the Oxford Movement, as distinct from the High Church reaction, is to be found.

II. *THE LEADERS KEBLE AND FROUDE*

THE DISCOVERY

I saw thee once, and nought descried
  For stranger to admire ;
A serious aspect, but it burned
  With no unearthly fire.

Again I saw, and I confessed
  Thy speech was rare and high ;
And yet it vexed my burdened breast,
  And scared, I knew not why.

I saw once more, and awestruck gazed
  On face, and form, and air ;
God's living glory round thee blazed—
  A saint—a saint was there !

J. H. N.,
Off Zante,
Jan. 8, 1833.

THAT Keble, Newman and Froude were the joint
authors and creators of the Oxford Movement few, if
any, students will deny, but it is a much more difficult
matter to determine their relative importance. Each
of them played an essential part, but no one of them
could have realized himself without the co-operation of
the rest. Froude alone would have gone up like a rocket
and left nothing behind him but a shower of sparks.
Keble alone would have been a Conservative county
clergyman who wrote pleasing religious verse and came
up to Oxford to vote against every reform. Newman
alone would certainly have done something, but who
can say what ? He might have been a leader of
Liberal opinion at Oxford or a great Evangelical
divine. He certainly would not have ended his days

as a cardinal of the Holy Roman Church. When Froude lay dying he compared himself to the murderer who had done one good act in his life and said that the one thing he had done was to bring Keble and Newman together and make them understand one another. And it is, in fact, difficult to exaggerate the importance of his contribution, for the contact of these two minds and wills, in the medium of Hurrell's sympathy, generated a new current of spiritual activity which transformed the religious life of England.

Of the three leaders, John Keble was the least original and the least creative. He represents the static element in the combination, and, partly on account of his seniority, both his character and his point of view were but little modified in the course of the movement. But for this very reason he supplied a solid *point d'appui* which such a movement requires. He was the last and in some respects the finest flower of the old Tory High Church tradition. He had grown up in the patriarchal atmosphere of his father Thomas Keble's parsonage, where, after the old fashion, he received his entire education up to his sixteenth year, when he entered the university ; and his whole life was spent in the " sacred seclusion of old English family life, among people enjoying a perfect harmony of taste and opinion." [1] He sacrificed a brilliant career at Oxford and the prospect of further advancement, in order to act as curate to his father in the Cotswolds and to look after him in his old age.

This devotion to his father finds its counterpart in his

[1] T. Mozley, *Reminiscences of Oriel College and the Oxford Movement*, I, p. 219.

attachment to the principle of loyalty in Church and State. The connexion comes out very clearly in his defence of the old Anglican doctrine of non-resistance, of which he is perhaps the last English apologist. " Obedience to rulers and magistrates," he says, " is in His judgement who cannot err, as sacred a duty as filial obedience and admits only of the same kind of exceptions. According to which, no calculations of expediency, no amount of private or public good, would justify a subject in violently resisting authority, except in such an extreme case as would justify a child under pupillage in violently resisting a father or mother." [1]

Hence Keble regards all indiscipline and insubordination, whether social, political or ecclesiastical, as essentially sinful and closely related to the vice of sensuality. " It is the same love of excitement and impatience of pure and quiet satisfactions ; venting itself, ordinarily, in wild and wanton pleasures ; and flaming out, when opportunity is given, in lawless defamation and rude resistance. These are the visible and actual results where men have audacity and ability to compass them : but who shall estimate the silent corruption which they daily and hourly foster in themselves, dreaming of and enjoying the mischief, which they want the heart or the power to realize." [2]

[1] *Sermons Academical and Occasional* (2nd ed., 1848), p. 112.
[2] *Ibid.*, p. 108.
Newman writes : " Keble was a man who guided himself and formed his judgements, not by processes of reason, by inquiry or by argument, but, to use the word in a broad sense, by authority. . . . What he hated instinctively was heresy, insubordination, resistance to things established, claims of independence, disloyalty, innovation, a critical censorious spirit." *Apologia*, p. 495 (ed. Ward, Oxford, 1913).

To a man with such convictions, whose nature was rooted so deeply in the past and who possessed so strong a sense of the sanctity of order and tradition, the shallow and self-confident rationalism of Benthamite Liberalism could not but be supremely distasteful. His tradition was that of Butler and the old English school of moral philosophy, but he developed this tradition in a more platonic and mystical sense than Shaftesbury or even Butler. In his eyes reason was always secondary : it was not a sufficient guide for human action, since it was incapable of reaching the foundations of moral life. To a far greater degree than the other leaders of the movement, Keble lived by an intuitive sense of spiritual realities and by the instinct which he terms " moral taste." It was by the cultivation of these spiritual instincts and not by the unbridled exercise of human intelligence that true knowledge was to be attained. It was a practical wisdom, like the Hokhma of the Old Testament writers, that was acquired only by obedience and conforming the mind and character to the norm of sacred tradition and to the Law of God.[1]

Thus the very intensity of Keble's religious sense led him to undervalue his own talents and deliberately to hide his intellectual gifts. As Dean Church has written, " it continually hampered the free play of his powers and gifts and made him often seem, to those who had not the key, awkward, unequal and unintelligible. But for this awful sense of power and reality unseen, which dwarfed to him all personal

[1] Cf. his sermon on *Favour shown to Implicit Faith* and the two succeeding sermons in *Sermons Academical and Occasional*.

thoughts and all present things, he might have been a
more finished writer, a more attractive preacher, a less
indifferent foster-father to his own works. But it
seemed to him a shame, in the presence of all that his
thoughts habitually dwelt with, to think of the ordinary
objects of authorship, of studying anything of this world
for its own sake, of perfecting works of art, of cultivating
the subtle forces and spells of language to give attrac-
tiveness to his writings. Abruptness, inadequacy and
obscurity of expression were light matters and gave
him little concern, compared with the haunting fear
of unreal words. This " seeking first the Kingdom of
God and His righteousness," as he understood it, was
the basis of all that he was ; it was really and un-
affectedly his governing principle, the root of his
affections and antipathies, just as is to other men the
passion for scientific discovery or political life." [1]

It is in Keble that the moral ideal of Tractarianism
finds its fullest expression. It is neither the mystical
spirituality of the Catholic tradition, nor the lush
emotional pietism of Evangelicalism, but a *via media* of
sanctity which has a severe beauty of its own. In
spite of its hostility to intellectualism, it was far from
undervaluing intellectual culture ; indeed it is intimately related to the tradition of Christian humanism
of which Keble himself was so perfect a representative.
This element is to be seen rather in Keble's remarkable
lectures on poetry [2] than in the more well-known
poetry of *The Christian Year*, which, as Froude com-

[1] *Occasional Papers*, by R. W. Church, Vol. II, p. 297 (1897).
[2] Cf. especially Keble's treatment of Virgil as a religious poet and
the concluding lecture on the natural harmony between Poetry and
true religion.

plained, is addressed not " to those who feel acutely,"
but " to plain matter-of-fact good sort of people,"
although even here it is by no means absent and has
contributed to make *The Christian Year* the classic of
Anglican devotional literature. It was, however, not
in his literary work but in his personal influence that
Keble's real power lay. Throughout its course
friendships played a great part in the history of the
Oxford Movement and Keble's leadership was due
above all to the personal affection that he inspired
among his disciples.

When in later years Newman came to know and
love the character of St. Philip Neri, it was to Keble
that his thoughts turned. " This great saint," he
wrote in 1847 to his sister, " reminds me in so many
ways of Keble that I can fancy what Keble would
have been if God's will had been that he should have
been born in another place and age ; he was formed
in the same type of extreme hatred of humbug, playful-
ness, nay, oddity, tender love for others, and severity,
which are lineaments of Keble." [1]

This power of personal influence is seen most clearly
in Keble's relations with his two pupils, Isaac Williams
and Hurrell Froude.

Isaac Williams always regarded his acquaintance
with Keble as the turning point in his life, and in his
autobiography he speaks in moving terms of the
profound impression made upon him by Keble's
character. " It was to me quite strange and wonderful
that one so distinguished should always ask one's
opinion as if he was younger than myself. And one so

[1] *Letters and Correspondence*, ed. by Anne Mozley (2nd ed.), II, p. 424.

overflowing with real genuine love in thought, word and action was quite new to me, I could scarcely understand it. . . . To find a person always endeavouring to do one good, as it were, unknown to oneself, and in secret, and even avoiding that his kindness should be felt and acknowledged as such, this opened upon me quite a new world. Religion a reality, and a man wholly made up of love, with charms of conversation, thought and knowledge, beyond what one had experienced among boyish companions—this broke in upon me all at once." [1]

No less profound was the impression produced by Keble on Hurrell Froude, though his instinctive dislike of sentimentality, or, as he used to call it, " sawniness," prevented him from expressing his feelings in the same way as Isaac Williams.

He came under the influence of Keble at a time of psychological crisis. The death of his charming and brilliant mother, Margaret Spedding, to whom he was passionately attached, had left him, to use his own words, as it were ἄθεος ἐν τῷ κόσμῳ, and in Keble he found a friend and a spiritual adviser who reorientated his mind in a religious direction and inspired him with a consuming passion for moral perfection. It may indeed be questioned whether Keble's method of spiritual guidance was a very prudent one, since it led him to follow a course of extreme asceticism and meticulous self-analysis which would have unsettled a weaker mind and which perhaps helped to weaken his constitution and to prepare the way for the disease which killed him. Nevertheless, wisdom is justified

[1] *Autobiography of Isaac Williams*, pp. 18–19.

of her children, and in spite of the apparently morbid scrupulosity of Froude's self-analysis and self-persecution, his asceticism was no mere negative repression ; it was a genuine training in moral fitness which worked off every ounce of superfluous tissue. It destroyed neither his sense of humour nor his intense spiritual vitality ; on the contrary it produced a sublimation of his natural qualities which became the more intense the more they were spiritualized. He is a living refutation of his own saying that " the cultivation of right principles has a tendency to make men dull and stupid." He was a lover of nature and poetry and horses and the sea : a bold rider and a brilliant talker, " who took his intellectual obstacles as he took his fences."

As his friend Lord Blachford wrote, " he had more of the undergraduate in him than any don whom I ever knew ; absolutely unlike Newman in being always ready to skate, sail or ride with his friends —and, if in a scrape, not pharisaical as to his means of getting out of it. I remember, *e.g.*, climbing Merton gate with him in my undergraduate days when we had been out too late boating or skating." [1] Above all, he was a gentleman, not in the Victorian sense of the word that was already coming into currency, but " according to that transcendental idea of the English gentleman which forms the basis of Toryism." " Luxury, show and even comfort he despised and denounced." " Self-renunciation in every form he could believe in ; most of all in a gentleman, particularly one of a good

---

[1] R. W. Church. *The Oxford Movement*, p. 51.

Devonshire family." [1]   He had the true aristocratic contempt of public opinion, and even, as his brother, James Antony notes, of private judgement, and a more than aristocratic generosity and regardlessness of self-interest.   In this he transcends the English aristocratic tradition and goes back to the parent tradition of European chivalry.   He was a gentleman of the stamp of Bayard and St. Louis, and he carried something of their spirit into the stuffy atmosphere of Oxford common rooms and into the ecclesiastical controversies of the age of the Reform Bill.   Like them, he despised success, and regarded wealth and talent and life itself as things not to be hoarded or enjoyed, but to be spent lavishly and cheerfully in the good cause.

It was this spirit of gallant self-spending, this super-naturalized chivalry, that, even more than his party loyalty and his vigorous thought, aroused the devotion of his friends and led them to regard him as the hero and champion of the movement.   There is a remarkable passage in an essay of one of the ablest of Tractarian writers, J. B. Mozley, in which the latter contrasts Froude with Thomas Arnold, the spiritual father of Victorianism, as the typical representatives of the two opposing systems.   " Singular it is," he writes, " that antagonist systems should so suit themselves with champions ; but if the world had been picked for the most fair, adequate and expressive specimens of German-religionism and catholicism—specimens that each side would have acknowledged—it could not well have produced better ones for the purpose than

[1] T. Mozley, *Reminiscences, Chiefly of Oriel College and the Oxford Movement,* I, pp. 226-227.

Dr. Arnold and Mr. Froude. Arnold, gushing with the richness of domestic life, the darling of nature, and overflowing receptacle and enjoyer, with strong healthy gusto, of all her endearments and sweets— Arnold, the representative of high, joyous Lutheranism, is describable—Mr. Froude hardly. His intercourse with earth and nature seemed to cut through them, like uncongenial steel, rather than mix and mingle with them. Yet the polished blade smiled as it went through. The grace and spirit with which he adorned this outward world, and seemed to an undiscerning eye to love it, were but something analogous in him to the easy tone of men in high life, whose good nature to their inferiors is the result either of their disinterested benevolence or of sublime unconcern. In him the severe sweetness of the life divine not so much rejected as disarmed those potent glows and attractions of the life natural: a high good temper civilly evaded and disowned them. The monk by nature, the born aristocrat of the Christian sphere, passed them clean by with inimitable ease ; marked his line and shot clear beyond them, into the serene ether, toward the far-off light, toward that needle's point on which ten thousand angels and all heaven moves." [1]

Such a character found a natural affinity in the pure and loyal spirit of John Keble. From the beginning their relations were unlike those of the ordinary master and pupil, or confessor and penitent.[2]

[1] J. B. Mozley, *Essays, Historical and Theological*, II, pp. 50–51. (Originally published in the *Christian Remembrancer*, Oct., 1844.)

[2] In 1825, when Froude was only twenty-two and Keble already possessed an unique reputation at Oxford, the latter sent him the MS. of the *Christian Year*, and Froude does not hesitate to point out that

Keble moulded Froude and inspired him with his own enthusiasm for the High Church and Cavalier tradition, and Froude in turn reacted on Keble and imparted some of his own vigour and combativeness to the elder man. Froude owed to Keble his high sense of religious values and his mystical view of life, but he raised Keble's ethical idealism to a more intense and meta-physical level. In spite of his lack of learning and philosophical training, his thought possesses real subtlety and depth. Starting from Keble's theory of " moral taste " as something analogous to the æsthetic sense, Froude conceived the mind as possessed of potentialities of spiritual vision that could be realized only by a process of moral ascesis which should gradu-ally shape the soul to harmony with the invisible realities of the world of faith. All through his papers this idea of *vision* is constantly recurring. Since " the blind part of the soul " possesses in the physical senses such amazing capacities for feeling, what must be the potentialities of the higher part of our nature, when once its spiritual blindness is removed ? " The varieties of that mysterious and unseen thing," he writes in 1827, " which is capable of pain and pleasure, between which we can now but faintly discriminate from observation of the various actions and opinions that they originate, may one day be objects of as distinct perception as are now the forms that are presented to our eyes. And the nameless faculty, whatever it may be, through which this perception shall be conveyed to us, may, like our personal organs of vision, be a

"there is something that I should call Sternhold-and-Hopkinsy in the diction." (*Remains*, I, p. 184.)

means of receiving delight as well as of discovering truth. . . ." [1]

Froude's philosophy, like his poetry, never attained adequate expression ; it belonged to the mysterious region of unrealized possibilities of which he wrote in some unfinished verses :

" The silent halls of Fate
Where lie in long and shadowy state
The embryos of the things that be
Waiting their hour of destiny." [2]

Nevertheless his friends always saw in him something very different from the brilliant and reckless controversialist that the world outside knew. Newman once described himself as the rhetorician and Froude and Keble as the philosophers of the movement, and on his death he wrote to Bowden, " I never, on the whole, fell in with so gifted a person. In variety and perfection of gifts I think he far exceeded even Keble. For myself, I cannot describe what I owe to him as regards the intellectual principles of religion and morals." [3]

Froude's natural atmosphere was not, as his critics often suppose, the atmosphere of theological controversy and party spirit, but the world of poetry and imagination. And in this he is representative of the movement which was formed in the atmosphere of prayer and poetry and found lyrical utterance before it began to express itself in tracts. Keble, Williams, Froude, Newman were all of them poets who looked to poetry for something more than æsthetic enjoyment, and to religion for something more than pious sentiment.

[1] *Remains*, I, p. 106 (April 13, 1827).
[2] *Ibid.*, I, p. 427 (1826).
[3] *Letters and Correspondence*, II, p. 156 (Mar. 2, 1836).

They held with Keble that " the very practice and cultivation of poetry will be found to possess, in some sort, the power of guiding the mind to worship and prayer." " For those who from their heart either burst into poetry or seek the Deity in prayer must needs ever cherish with their whole spirit the vision of something more beautiful, greater and more lovable than all that mortal eye can see." [1]

Thus the roots of the Oxford Movement are to be found not so much in Oxford itself as in the county parsonages of Gloucestershire and Devon, by the banks of the Windrush and the Dart. It was there that the first links were forged of the chain that was to draw the Anglican tradition out of the rut of conventionality and Erastianism in which it had stuck so long. Dartington to-day hums with activity ; the old Church has been destroyed and the Froudes' home has become a parochial centre. But on the other bank of the Dart, in the woods of Little Hempston, there still stands the little 14th century manor house, which Hurrell regarded as the most beautiful place in the world, with its effaced fresco of the mystery of the Resurrection, a memorial at once of Froude himself and of the old Catholic England to which he had pledged his faith.

[1] *Lectures on Poetry*, tr. E. K. Francis (1912), II, pp. 482–483.

III. *NEWMAN AND THE EVANGELICAL TRADITION*

MELCHIZEDEK

Thrice blest are they who feel their loneliness ;
To whom nor voice of friend nor pleasant scene
Brings that on which the saddened heart can lean ;
Yea the rich earth, garbed in its daintiest dress
Of light and joy, doth but the more oppress,
Claiming responsive smiles and raptures high :
Till sick at heart behind the veil they fly,
Seeking His presence, Who alone can bless.
Such in strange days, the weapons of Heaven's grace ;
When passing o'er the high-born Hebrew line,
He forms the vessel of his vast design ;
Fatherless, homeless, reft of age and place,
Severed from earth and careless of its wreck,
Born through long woe His rare Melchizedek.

J. H. N.,
Corfu,
Jan. 5, 1833.

As the friendship between Keble and Froude prepared the way for the Oxford Movement, so that between Froude and Newman made it a reality. It is difficult to exaggerate the importance of Froude's influence on Newman during the years from 1829 to 1836 which saw the inauguration of the movement and the ripening of Newman's own genius. As Dr. Abbott has written, " Froude (not Froude's opinions, but Froude himself, or his personality, Froude, first living, and then, as a posthumous influence, still more powerful after death) did more than any other external thing to make Newman what he became, and to shape, through Newman, the Tractarian Movement." [1] Not

---

[1] *The Anglican Career of Cardinal Newman*, by Edwin A. Abbott, 1892.

that this detracts in any real sense from Newman's greatness and originality. In intellectual genius and in the power of spiritual leadership Newman stands so far above all the other members of the group as almost to justify James Anthony Froude's expression " compared with him they were all as ciphers and he the indicating number." [1] It was the genius of Newman that gave the movement its high intellectual character and at the same time immeasurably widened its spirit and its aims. As Dr. Brilioth has pointed out, he represents the dynamic element in the movement, as opposed to the static element represented by the old High Church party ; indeed, it was this dynamic quality in his personality which gave him his peculiar power of assimilating the ideas and the ethos of men so unlike himself as Froude and Keble and incorporating them in the vital development of his religious experience. He was not like the other leaders, a born Tory and High Churchman who was committed by heredity and cultural tradition to the defence of Anglican ideals. He did not belong, like them, to the agrarian England of the squires and parsons, but to the new middle class which was beginning to supplant the latter in the leadership of English culture. This class was naturally alien to the High Church tradition. It tended to be Liberal in politics and in ideas, and it was mainly responsible for the great reforming movement of which the High Church party was the sworn enemy and against which the Oxford Movement itself was a conscious reaction.

[1] *Short Studies*, IV. "The Oxford County—Reformation," I, p. 157.

Nevertheless this class was as a whole intensely religious. It possessed its own religious traditions, which were no less deeply rooted in the national tradition than that of the High Church and possessed a far stronger hold on English character.[1] This tradition had its roots in the Puritanism of the 17th century and in the Methodism of the 18th and ultimately in the Calvinist Reformation, though it also contained elements derived from Lutheran pietism and from the lesser sects. In the early 17th century it was represented by the Evangelical Movement, which seemed to embody all that was living and active in the religious life of the time. Its influence made itself felt in the most diverse quarters—among the cultured bankers and politicians of the Clapham group, and among county labourers and the swarming masses of the new industrial towns, among learned and saintly Anglican clergy, such as Thomas Scott, Charles Simeon and the Milners, as well as among the fanatics and adventurers of the type of Joanna Southcott.

It was responsible not only for the movement of

[1] Of course we must not forget the existence of devout High Churchmen, such as Joshua Watson and William Stevens among the middle classes, or the fact that the Evangelical movement made converts like Lady Huntingdon, Alexander Knox, Lord Teignmouth and Lord Shaftesbury, among the upper classes. The latter, however, tended on the whole to look askance at Evangelicalism as we see from the Duchess of Buckingham's famous letter to Lady Huntingdon : " I thank your ladyship for the information concerning the Methodist preachers, their doctrines are most repulsive and strongly tinctured with impertinence and disrespect towards their superiors in perpetually endeavouring to level all ranks and do away with all distinctions. It is monstrous to be told you have a heart as sinful as the common wretches that crawl on the earth. This is highly offensive and insulting ; and I cannot but wonder that your ladyship should relish any sentiments as much at variance with high rank and good breeding. I shall be most happy to come and hear your favourite preacher."—Gledstone's *Life of Whitefield*, p. 304.

popular religious revival, which perhaps, as M. Halévy maintains, saved England from the danger of revolution, but also for the great humanitarian movement which abolished the slave trade and laid the foundations of modern social reform. But its real strength lay neither in the emotional appeal of its preachers and revivalists nor in the external activity of its philanthropists. Behind all this there was the force of genuine intellectual conviction and the massive solidity of the Calvinistic theology which, as Newman points out in his essay on the Countess of Huntingdon, could impress even unbelievers like Lord Bolingbroke, who had nothing but contempt for the ethical platitudes of the Broad Church divines.[1]

Calvinism to-day is almost completely *terra incognita* to the ordinary educated Englishman. We see the mark that it has left on history, but we no longer understand its spirit. It is like the bed of a dry torrent whose cliffs and boulders bear witness to the gigantic force of which it was once the channel. Nevertheless Calvinism has much more in common with the religion of Newman, and indeed with Catholicism itself, than the Erastian conservatism of the old High Church tradition.[2] It has a far higher and clearer sense of the supernatural order and of its

[1] Newman, *Essays Critical and Historical*, I, pp. 402–403.
[2] This was partially recognized by Hurrell Froude himself. " Calvinism," he writes, " amidst all its errors had two truths. Though its Articles of Faith were erroneous, yet it asserted that a true faith was necessary to salvation, and though its discipline was a human invention, yet it asserted that Church authority was from God. Against these two truths of Calvinism were forged the doctrines of Arminius and Erastus ; the former asserting that mere opinions were matters of indifference, and the latter that the Church was a mere creature of the State." *Remains*, III, p. 394.

transcendent character. The distinction between
"the Church" and "the world," between "the
saints" or "the elect" and the unregenerate, is all-
important and governs the whole Calvinistic conception of life. It manifests itself both in its view of
history, which is conceived after the manner of St.
Augustine as the evolution of two contrary principles
embodied in two hostile societies, Jerusalem and
Babylon, the city of God and the city of the Devil, and
in the severe asceticism of its ethical ideal and its
refusal to rest satisfied with easy-going standards and
an external acceptance of Christianity. This thorough-
going supernaturalism shows itself above all in the
Calvinist idea of the Church as a free and autonomous
society, which controlled the lives of its members down
to the minutest particulars and rejected all interference
on the part of the secular power. In the great age of
Calvinism the ideal assumed a thoroughly theocratic
form, and its representatives laid down the law to
princes and asserted "the Crown rights of Christ" as
uncompromisingly as any mediæval pontiff.

Thus Calvinism agrees with Catholicism in its three
fundamental principles—the supernatural order, the
supernatural society and the supernatural life. But it
interprets these principles in a spirit of sectarian rigidity
which entirely alters their meaning. Calvinism, like
Catholicism, accepted the Augustinian theology of
grace, but divested it of its mystical and sacramental
elements. Hence its ethical ideal acquired the harsh
and unamiable features that made Puritanism so
unpopular. Hence, too, the bareness of its liturgy and
the aridity of its dogmatism. Above all, its assertion

of the complete corruption of human nature destroyed the Catholic hierarchy of nature and supernature and substituted a sharp dualism which led to the impoverishment of culture and to the narrowing of the intellectual outlook of Calvinism.

These defects all appear in an accentuated form in the English Evangelical tradition. Its outward appearance was unattractive, as we see not only in the Bethels and Ebenezers of the sects, but even more in the proprietary chapels of the fashionable Evangelical preachers. And this material ugliness is by no means altogether irrelevant, for it is the outward sign of a certain spiritual unattractiveness—a lack of *grace*—which points to a vital defect in the religious life of the movement. Even at its best, English Evangelicalism lacked sweetness and light, and was largely responsible, as Matthew Arnold pointed out, for the Philistinism of the British middle class, while at its worst it sank to appalling depths of cant and hypocrisy. The most serious indictment of English Evangelicalism is to be found not in the writings of its theological opponents, but in the work of contemporary secular men of letters, above all the great Victorian novelists. If Trollope does not spare the worldliness and Erastianism of the old High Church tradition as represented by Archdeacon Grantley, the latter is an angel of light in comparison with the reptilian loathsomeness of Mr. Slope.

No doubt Mr. Slope is a caricature, but there was much in the Evangelical movement that lent itself to such caricature ; that explains the disfavour with which the Evangelicals were regarded in conservative circles.

If we may believe Newman's brother-in-law, the
position of the Evangelical party at Oxford in the
reign of George IV. was not unlike that of Mr. Slope at
Barchester.[1] " It is difficult to convey an idea of the
very low position that it had in the university ; and
it is even painful to recall it for it was religion in the
form of a degradation utterly undeserved. There were
in most of the other colleges (besides St. Edmund's
Hall) one or two men who inherited or imbibed
sympathy with the despised sect. But to Whately in
his lofty eminence of free speculation the Evangelical
system as presented at Oxford was below contempt." [2]

It was impossible that Newman with his intense
æsthetic sensibility and his strong and subtle intelligence
should remain permanently bound by the limited
ideas of the Evangelical tradition. He had grown up
in the rather drab surroundings of the pre-Victorian
bourgeoisie and had received from the teaching of an
Evangelical schoolmaster those first religious impressions which were never to be effaced or obscured.
Newman never forgot what he owed to his early
Evangelical teachers and to the writings of men like
Thomas Scott, Doddridge, Romaine and the Milners.
He always regarded this first conversion as the turning
point in his life, and fifty years later he was to speak of
it as something " of which I am still more certain than
that I have hands or feet." During his first years at
Oxford, and even as late as 1824, Newman was strictly
Evangelical in his ideas and used the conventional

'How is it," he asks, " that goodness, poverty and a certain
amount of literary or religious ambition, produce an unpleasant effect
on the skin ? " *Reminiscences*, by T. Mozley, I, p. 243.

[2] *Reminiscences*, I, pp. 23–24.

language of Evangelical pietism. He describes Dr. Pusey in 1823 as " a searching man," and prays that he may be brought " into the true Church." " How can I doubt his seriousness ? " he asks (rather unnecessarily, one might have supposed). " His very eagerness to talk of the Scriptures seems to prove it. May I lead him forward, at the same time gaining good from him." And again : " That Pusey is Thine, O Lord, how can I doubt ? . . . Yet I fear he is prejudiced against Thy children. Let me never be eager to convert him to a *party* or to a form of opinion." [1]

Certainly no one could doubt young Mr. Newman's seriousness, and this together with his extreme shyness made him at first a lonely and silent member of his new college. At this time Oriel was the stronghold of the Oxford intelligentsia, and its fellows had a reputation for hard talking and loud argument which was not calculated to put a shy man at his ease. Unfriendly critics said that Oriel common room " stank of logic," and Samuel Wilberforce, a decade later, gave his impressions of it in a few blistering lines which would be still more effective if we could insert the names which his biographer has thought fit to expunge. " I dined in common room where the sights and sounds were curious : the cantankerous conceit of ——, ——'s pettishness, the vulgar priggishness of ——'s jokes ; the loud ungentlemanliness of ——'s cut lip arguments ; the disinterred liveliness of —— and the silence of Newman were all *surprenant*, nay *épouvantable*." [2]

Such society might seem the last thing to cure

---

[1] *Letters and Correspondence*, I, p. 103.
[2] *Life of Bishop Samuel Wilberforce*, I, p. 86 (Nov. 10, 1835.)

Newman of his shyness and reserve. Nevertheless he was cured by the loudest and the most argumentative of them all : Dr. Whately. The latter was one of the most original and formidable figures of later Georgian Oxford, one of those

> " Regal dons
> With heart of gold and lungs of bronze."

whose praises Mr. Belloc has written.

He had a gargantuan appetite, both for food and argument, and used to boast that he used his friends as anvils to beat out his ideas. He had an equal contempt for the High Church and the Evangelicals, whom he described as the Sadducees and the Pharisees. One can hardly imagine a more incongruous couple than this burly philosopher who was never tired of the sound of his own voice, and sensitive and self-absorbed young Newman, who used to suffer agonies at the thought of the imaginary solecism he had committed in conversation. Nevertheless, in spite of the severity with which Whately criticized his theological views, Newman became his devoted disciple.

Under the bracing stimulus of Whately's intercourse, which he compares to a March north-easter tempered by a June sun, Newman learnt for the first time to think for himself—" to see with my own eyes and to stand on my own feet." This was Newman's second spiritual awakening—a purely intellectual one, and it seemed for a time as though the Oriel school of Anglican Liberalism had gained in him a distinguished and promising recruit. They little realized that they were training one who was to be the most formidable opponent of the cause of Liberalism that Oxford ever

knew. In later years Copleston used to apply to Newman the lines from the *Agamemnon* of Æschylus about the
tame lion cub which seems a nice pet for the children
until, as it grows, it reveals the fount of fierceness
whence it came.

> A curse they nursed for their own undoing,
> A mouth by which their own friends shall perish,
> A servant of Ate, a priest of Ruin,
> Some god hath taught them to cherish.

Newman's transformation from the promising young
Liberal don, who was Whately's disciple, to the leader
of the reaction to Liberalism belongs to the years
1826—1829, and was almost exclusively due to the
influence of Hurrell Froude. It was in 1826 that the
latter was elected to an Oriel fellowship and the two
young men were attracted to one another from the
first, in spite of the sharp opposition between their
religious opinions and social traditions. In the years
when Newman had been sitting at the feet of Whately,
Froude had been sitting at the feet of Keble, but for
all the difference in their teachers their intellectual
training possessed one thing in common. Both of
them had owed their philosophy of religion to Bishop
Butler and both of them were born Platonists who
interpreted Butler's Christian pragmatism in the spirit
of Christian Platonism. Newman has described how
he learnt from Butler to view the natural and visible
world as sacramentally connected with the invisible
world of spirit on which it was dependent, and this
was the same principle which Froude had imbibed
from Keble. In the same way Newman learnt from
Butler to view conscience as the supreme organ of

religious consciousness, the spiritual faculty which opens the eyes of the mind to the truths of faith ; and here again we have the same principle of the moral sense which held so large a place in the thought of Keble and Froude.

Apart from this common intellectual foundation, Froude quickly recognized in Newman an originality and brilliancy of intellect that contrasted with the ponderous and unattractive minds of the older dons like Davidson. Immediately after his election he wrote to Keble " (Newman) is to my mind by far the greatest genius of the party, and I cannot help thinking that some time or other I may get to be well acquainted with him." [1] Newman, on the other hand, found in Froude a more brilliant and stimulating intelligence than any he had hitherto known. As Whately's influence had freed him from the narrow pietism of his Evangelistic past, so now Froude liberated him from the shallow and unimaginative intellectualism of contemporary Liberalism with which he had no fundamental sympathy. And while intercourse with Whately was an exhausting affair of hammer and anvil, Froude conducted his controversies with the exhilarating speed and zest of an intellectual sportsman. " Woe to anyone who dropped in his hearing such phrases as the Dark Ages, superstition, bigotry, right of private judgement, enlightenment, ' march of mind,' or progress . . . it was as if a fox had broken cover ; there ensued a chase and no mercy." [2]

At first, no doubt, Newman must have been shocked

---

[1] *Remains*, I, p. 199.
[2] Mozley's *Reminiscences*, I, p. 226.

by Froude's startling paradoxes and by his defiance of
accepted opinion, while Froude was equally scandalized
by Newman's " heresy." " He is a fellow," he writes
to Keble in 1828, " that I like the more, the more I
think of him ; only I would give a few odd pence if he
were not a heretic ! " Nevertheless, there was latent
in Newman the same intellectual recklessness and
daring that were characteristic of Froude, and it only
needed the stimulus of the latter's intercourse to bring
them to the surface. Both men shared the same love
of speculation, the same fearlessness of consequences
and even a certain fierceness of spirit that led them to
despise compromise and to defy the prejudices of the
majority. The result of this is to be seen in Newman's
breach with Whately and the Liberals and his going
over to Keble and the reactionaries on the question of
Sir Robert Peel's election in 1829. It was not that
Newman was hostile to Catholic Emancipation, for he
was still a rather luke-warm supporter of the measure.
But he felt, like Keble, that Peel's abrupt change of
views was a sacrifice of principles to political expediency
and he was not sorry to have an opportunity of showing
his independence of a party which claimed to represent
" the talent of the university." In a remarkable letter
written to his mother after the election, he explains his
new attitude to Liberalism and his fears of an approach-
ing crisis which would separate the Church from the
State and leave the upper classes almost without
religion.

" The talent of the day is against the Church. The
Church party (visibly at least, for there may be latent
talent, and great times give birth to great men) is poor

in mental endowments. It has not activity, shrewdness, dexterity, eloquence, practical power. On what, then, does it depend ? On prejudice and bigotry.

" This is hardly an exaggeration, yet I have good meaning and one honourable to the Church. Listen to my theory. As each individual has certain instincts of right and wrong antecedently to reasoning, on which he acts—and rightly so—which perverse reasoning may supplant, which then can hardly be regained, but if regained will be regained from a different source— from reasoning, not from nature—so, I think has the world of men collectively, God gave them truths in His miraculous revelations, and other truths in the un-sophisticated infancy of nations, scarcely less necessary and divine. These are transmitted as ' the wisdom of our ancestors ' through men, many of whom cannot enter into them, or receive them themselves—still on, on from age to age, not the less truths because many of the generations through which they are transmitted are unable to prove them, but hold them, either from pious and honest feeling (it may be), or from bigotry or from prejudice. That they are truths it is most difficult to prove, for great men alone can prove great ideas or grasp them. Such a mind was Hooker's, such Butler's ; and as moral evil triumphs over good on a small field of action, so in the argument of an hour or the compass of a volume would men like Brougham, or again Wesley, show to far greater advantage than Hooker or Butler. Moral truth is gained by patient study, by calm reflection, silently as the dew falls— unless miraculously given—and when gained it is transmitted by faith and by ' prejudice.' Keble's book is full of such truths, which any Cambridge man might refute with the greatest ease." [1]

This traditionalism, which so strikingly resembles the traditionalism of de Bonald and the other thinkers of the French Catholic revival, marks the starting point of Newman's philosophy, and it undoubtedly bears the mark of Froude's influence. He had already come to know and love Keble, and he rapidly assimilated the prejudices and loyalties of his new friends, in his country walks and rides with Froude. " Shotover," he writes to Bowden, " is in our minds quite a classical place ; especially, as Milton once lived near it, before he was contaminated by evil times and the waywardness of a proud heart ; and King Charles and his Bishops seemed to rise before us along the old road which leads from Oxford to Cuddesdon. We have been paying a good deal of attention to the history of these times, and I am confirmed as a dull, staid Tory, unfit for these smart times. Which way is the world marching ? and how *we* shall be left behind when the movement is ordered by the word of command ! " [2]

But Newman's sympathy with the romantic loyalties of Keble and Froude was a comparatively superficial and temporary element in his change of views. His hostility to Liberalism had far deeper roots than the High Church Toryism of his friends. It was due to his sense of the essential falsity of the Liberal and Utilitarian philosophy when brought face to face with the facts of life. Newman had a profound sense of the reality of evil and suffering—of the dark mystery

[1] *Letters and Correspondence*, I, pp. 179–180.
[2] *Ibid.*, I, p. 195 (Jan. 16, 1830).

of human existence which the self-satisfied optimism of the party of progress ignored so completely. Which is the true view of human nature and human history— that of the Liberals and the Utilitarians or that of the Hebrew prophets ? Does the destiny of mankind depend on the progress of science and the growth of representative institutions, or does it lie in the shadow of the mystery of Divine judgement ? These were the questions that Newman set himself to face and his answer is to be found in that remarkable series of sermons which first revealed to the Oxford of 1832 that a prophet had risen up among them. These are directed not so much against Liberalism in its more extreme and openly anti-Christian forms as against those who attempted to adopt Christianity to the spirit of the age—to make it a religion of universal benevolence and to hide or explain away its darker and deeper aspects. " They have healed the wound of the daughter of my people slightly, saying, Peace, peace, when there is no peace." Against what he calls the "flimsy, self-invented notions which satisfy the reason of the mere man of letters or prosperous and self-indulgent philosopher," he sets the spectacle of " the overwhelming total of the world's guilt and suffering, suffering crying for vengeance on the authors of it, and guilt forboding it." The real religion of nature is not to be found in the optimistic platitudes of Deism but in the dark and bloody superstitions of the heathen. " Doubtless these desperate and dark struggles are to be called superstition when viewed by the side of true religion ; and it is easy enough to speak of them as superstition, when we have been informed of the gracious and joyful result in which the scheme of Divine Governance issues. But it is man's truest and best religion, *before* the Gospel shines on him. If our race *be* in a fallen and depraved state, what ought our religion to be but anxiety and remorse till God comfort us ? Surely to be in gloom—to view ourselves with horror—to look about to the right hand and to the left for means of safety—to catch at everything, yet trust in nothing—to do all we can, and try to do more than all—and, after all, to wait in miserable suspense, naked and shivering, among the trees of the garden, for the hour of His coming, and meanwhile to fancy sounds of woe in every wind stirring the leaves about us—in a word, to be superstitious—is nature's best offering, her most acceptable service, her most mature and enlarged wisdom, in the presence of a holy and offended God." [1]

And as Newman sets this true natural religion of fallen man against the sham " natural religion " of the philosophers, so too he contrasts the living power of historic Christianity with the abstract moralism which was all that human reason could offer to the needs of humanity. " Such then is the Revealed system compared with the Natural—teaching religious truths historically, not by investigation ; revealing the Divine nature not in works but in action ; not in His moral laws, but in His spoken commands, training us to be subjects of a kingdom, not citizens of a stoic republic, and enforcing obedience, not on Reason, so much as on Faith." [2] The meaning of history is not

[1] *University Sermons* (1843), pp. 105–106. " On Justice as a principle of Divine Governance."
[2] *University Sermons*, p. 32. " The Influence of Natural and Revealed Religion Respectively."

to be found by human reason or in human civilization. It moves to a supernatural and divine goal, a goal which is to be reached not by the progress of civilization and science but by the fostering of a divine seed which will bear an eternal flower.

> These are the chosen few,
> The remnant fruit of largely-scattered grace.
> God sows in waste, to reap whom He foreknew
>   Of man's cold race,
> Counting on wills perverse, in His clear view
>   Of boundless time and space,
> He waits, by scant return for treasures given
>   To fill the thrones of heaven.[1]

" The main undertaking of a Christian Church " is not according to the notion of the day " to make men good members of society, honest, upright, industrious and well-conducted," but to make saints, to form those rare, hidden souls who are the heirs of the world to come. And it does this " not as a system, not by books, not by argument, nor by temporal power," but by the handing on of the seed of life from man to man and from age to age.

It is noteworthy that Newman's emphasis here is not on the hierarchical principle of episcopal succession, but on the more mystical idea of an Apostolic succession of saints. Few as they are, " they are enough to carry on God's noiseless work. The Apostles were such men ; others might be named in their several generations as successors to their holiness. These communicate their light to a number of lesser luminaries by whom in its turn it is distributed through the world ; the first sources of illumination being all the while unseen, even by the majority of sincere Christians—

[1] *Lyra Apostolica*, LV. " The True Elect."

unseen as is that Supreme Author of Light and Truth from whom all good primarily proceeds."

Hence it is useless for the Liberal to invoke " the spirit of the age," or " the progress of society," or " the march of mind " in order to overawe the opposition of the Christian. All this imposing progress is but the movement of a dying world sweeping onwards to inevitable destruction. " Even though the march of society be conducted on a superhuman law (such as the law of progress), yet, while it moves against Scripture Truth, it is not God's ordinance—it is but the creature of Satan ; and, though it shiver all earthly obstacles to its progress, the gods of Sepharvaim and Arphad, fall it must, and perish it must, before the glorious Fifth Kingdom of the Most High, when He visits the earth who is called Faithful and True, whose eyes are as a flame of fire and on His head many crowns, who smites the nations with a rod of iron and treadeth the winepress of fierceness and wrath of Almighty God." [1]

This was a strange voice in the Oxford of 1832, where the atmosphere of the 18th century, with its fear of enthusiasm and fanaticism and superstition still lingered, but it was not strange to the religious consciousness of the British people. It might have found an echo on many a Scotch hillside and in many an English village wherever the Puritan tradition was still alive. For it is the fundamental doctrine of Calvinism divested of its sectarian exaggerations and of the jargon of Evangelistic pietism and brought back to its Augustinian and Biblical origins. To find

[1] *University Sermons* (1st ed.), p. 142.

Newman's spiritual ancestors we must look not, as with Keble, to the spiritual leaders of High Church Anglicanism of the school of Laud and Ken and Wilson, but to the great Puritan divines such as Thomas Goodwin, above all, who most of all resembles Newman in certain aspects of his teaching.[1] He inherited this tradition and he desectarianized it, shedding one by one the peculiar tenets of final perseverance, of the assurance of salvation, of the apprehension of Christ and of Imputation, which narrowed and distorted Evangelical religion.[2] What gave Newman his unique power as the leader of the Oxford Movement and the reformer of the Anglican Church was the fact that he was not merely the champion of a theory of ecclesiastical order, but the teacher of a theology of grace. Throughout his life, as he wrote in his last days to the secretary of the London Evangelical Society,[3] his mind was possessed by those " great and burning truths which [he] learned when a boy from Evangelical teaching," which he taught when a man at Oxford,

[1] Cf., for example, Goodwin's sermon preached before the House of Commons on Feb. 25, 1645, on *The Great Interest of States and Kingdoms* with Newman's *Sermons on Subjects of the Day*, especially those on *The Christian Church an Imperial Power*.

[2] " He used to say that whereas upon that great change that took place in him as a boy there were four doctrines all of which he held as if certain truths—namely, those of the Holy Trinity, of the Incarnation, of Predestination, and of the Lutheran apprehension of Christ—the first three, which are doctrines of the Catholic religion, . . . remained indelible through all his changes of opinion, up to and over the date of his becoming a Catholic ; whereas the fourth, which is not true, though he thought it was, . . . did in the event, as is the nature of a mere opinion or untrue belief, take its departure from his mind in a very short time . . ." *Autobiographical Memoir* in *Letters and Correspondence*, I, p. 110. Cp. *Apologia* (ed. Ward, Oxford, 1913), pp. 108–110, when he also notes the influence on his mind down to 1843 of the Calvinistic view of the Pope as Antichrist.

[3] Ward, *Life of Newman*, II, p. 527 (Feb. 1887).

and which he found at last shining in their true glory
in the Catholic Roman Church.[1]

[1] It is noteworthy that the precursor of the Oxford Movement,
Alexander Knox, should like Newman have derived his religious
inspiration from Evangelicalism and should have been led towards
Catholicism in consequence of his study of the theology of grace and by
his sense of the inadequacy of the current Protestant doctrine of imputation. He was, however, an unsystematic and eclectic thinker who
found the solution of his problem in the formula—Protestant justification + Catholic sanctification.

IV. *THE MEDITERRANEAN JOURNEY*

THE GOOD SAMARITAN

O that thy creed were sound !
For thou dost soothe the heart, thou Church of Rome,
By thy unwearied watch and varied round
Of service, in thy Saviour's holy home.
I cannot walk the city's sultry streets,
But the wide porch invites to still retreats,
Where passion's thirst is calmed, and care's unthankful gloom.

There on a foreign shore,
The home-sick solitary finds a friend :
Thoughts, prisoned long for lack of speech, outpour
Their tears ; and doubts in resignation end.
I almost fainted at the long delay,
That tangles me within this languid bay,
When comes a foe, my wounds with oil and wine to tend.

J. H. N.,
June 13, 1833.

[Written by Newman after his illness in Sicily. " I was aching to get home " he says, "yet for want of a vessel I was kept at Palermo for three weeks. I began to visit the Churches and they calmed my impatience, though I did not attend any services." *Apologia*, p. 135.]

WE have seen how the Evangelical element in Newman's religion expressed itself in a profoundly supernatural conception of Christianity, and distinguishes his reaction against Liberalism from the traditional conservatism of the official High Church party and from the romantic idealism of Keble and Froude. But there is another element in his thought which explains his conversion to the High Church tradition and his sympathy with the Anglican theologians of the 17th century. This was his love of Catholic antiquity which, strangely enough, he had

45

learnt from his early Evangelical teachers,[1] but which received a new meaning in the light of the principles which he acquired from Froude and Keble in 1829. Already in his sermons of that year we find a new realization of the divine prerogative of the Church—" not an institution of man, not a creature of the State, depending on the State's breath, made and unmade at its will, but a Divine society, a great work of God, a true relic of Christ and His Apostles, as Elijah's mantle on Elisha, a bequest which He has left us and which we must keep for His sake "[2]

This vision of the Church " bright as the sun and terrible as an army set in array " was indeed far removed from the prosaic reality of the Hanoverian Establishment. All the greater, then, was Newman's delight when, in 1831–32, his studies on the ecclesiastical history of the 4th century revealed to him the Church of the Fathers in all its glory. There at last he found the religious ideal that he had looked for in vain in Evangelical pietism and in the intellectualism of Whately and the " Noetics," a religion that was spiritual without emotionalism and intellectual without rationalism—a Church that was the temple of super-rational wisdom and supernatural holiness. Here too in the Christian Platonism of the Alexandrian and Cappadocian Fathers he found the complete justification of the mysticism which was characteristic of the early Tractarians and which Newman shared with Keble and Froude and Isaac Williams and J. B. Morris

[1] From The *Church History* of Joseph Milner, which he read as early as 1816.
[2] *Parochial and Plain Sermons*, VII, xvii, p. 242 (Nov., 1829). Cp. III, xiv, " On Submission to Church Authority " (Nov., 1829).

—a mysticism which regards all earthly things as types and shadows of the invisible reality which lies hidden behind them. " What we see is the outward shell of an eternal kingdom ", within lies hidden the real world : a world of Saints and Angels, a glorious world, the palace of God, the mountain of the Lord of Hosts, the heavenly Jerusalem, the throne of God and Christ, all these wonders, everlasting, all-precious, mysterious and incomprehensible lie hidden in what we see." [1] The Church is the hierophant of this Divine Mystery, and in her the realities of the invisible world become visible and tangible to human experience. And consequently ecclesiastical dogmas are not to be judged or justified by human reason ; they are all of reality that we can know, the fixed stars that shine in the obscurity of a world of shadows.

Such doctrines made a deep impression on Newman's mind, which had far more in common with the spirit of Athanasius and Basil than with that of Paley or Sydney Smith. In the Church of the Christian East with its depth of theological speculation and its warmth of ascetic devotion he found his ideal of what a Christian Church should be and by this standard he judged the Anglican Church of his own day and found it wanting. As he writes in the *Apologia*, " With the Establishment thus divided and threatened, thus ignorant of its true strength, I compared that fresh vigorous power of which I was reading in the first centuries. In her triumphant zeal on behalf of that Primeval Mystery, to which I had had so great a devotion from my youth, I recognized the movement of my spiritual Mother. *Incessu patuit Dea.*

[1] *Parochial Sermons*, III, xiii, " The Invisible World."

The self-conquest of her Ascetics, the patience of her Martyrs, the irresistible determination of her Bishops, the joyous swing of her advance, both exalted and abashed me. I said to myself, ' Look on this picture and on that ' ; I felt affection for my own Church, but not tenderness ; I felt dismay at her prospects, anger and scorn at her do-nothing perplexity. I thought that if Liberalism once got a footing within her, it was sure of the victory in the event. I saw that Reformation principles were powerless to rescue her. As to leaving her, the thought never crossed my imagination ; still I ever kept before me that there was something greater than the Established Church, and that that was the Church Catholic and Apostolic, set up from the beginning, of which she was but the local presence and the organ. She was nothing, unless she was this. She must be dealt with strongly, or she would be lost. There was need of a second Reformation " [1]

Meanwhile Hurrell Froude had reached the same conclusion by a different but even more direct path. About the same time that Newman was discovering the Church of the Fathers, Froude was discovering the Reformation, and his discovery filled him with disgust and astonishment. What Froude had learned from Keble was not so much a theology as an ethical attitude and an historical tradition, and it was in this spirit that he approached the subject. He set out to study the ethos of the reformers rather than their doctrines, and he soon came to the conclusion that their ethos was profoundly unsatisfactory. Instead of

[1] *Apologia* (ed. Ward), p. 132.

venerable divines, such as Andrewes and Sancroft and
Ken, he found himself in the presence of men who
seemed to possess all the qualities that Keble had
taught him to abhor. They despised tradition, they
had no reverence for the past, they fawned on the
secular power, and they attacked the most sacred
mysteries of Catholic worship with scurrilous invective.
If such men were right, then all that Keble stood for
was mistaken. If men like Luther and Jewel were not
heretics, then it was clear that no such thing as an
heretical ethos existed.

Thus Froude came to realize, almost from the
beginning, that Protestantism and Catholicism are
not two elements that can be blended in varying
proportions in a composite body, but two different
religions based on diametrically opposite principles.
It was no use to halt between two opinions. " If the
Lord was God follow Him, but if Baal then follow him."
When once Froude had made up his mind, there
were no half measures, and for the last four years of
his life he made it his mission to explode the myth of
" our glorious Reformation " and to indoctrinate his
friends with his own views. " Why do you praise
Ridley ? " he asks Newman in 1835. " Do you know
sufficient good about him to counterbalance the fact
that he was the associate of Cranmer, Peter Martyr
and Bucer ? (N.B.—How beautifully the *Edinburgh
Review* has shown up Luther, Melanchthon and Co. !
What good genius has possessed them to do our dirty
work ?) I have also to grumble at you for letting Pusey
call the Reformers ' the Founders of our Church,' in
that excellent and much-to-be-studied work on Fasting

(*Tract* 18). *Pour moi*, I never mean, if I can help it, to use any phrases even, which can connect me with such a set. I shall never call the Holy Eucharist ' the Lord's Supper,' nor God's priests ' Ministers of the Word,' nor the Altar ' the Lord's Table,' etc., etc. ; innocent as such phrases are in themselves, they have been dirtied ; a fact of which you seem oblivious on many occasions." [1]

In all this Froude was the moving spirit, and Newman and Keble were dragged on half against their will. But he could claim with some justification that he was only making them know their own minds and realize the bearing of their own principles. He was once asked how it was that he had come to hate the Reformers as he did, and he replied that it was as soon as he began to know ——? Newman or Keble.[2] " I felt they were the very kind of fellows he would most have hated and despised if he had known them. But I did not dare to sport my opinions till I had read more and got him to agree with me. I believe I have a want of reverence, else I should not have got to hate them as soon as I did. —— used sometimes to give

---

[1] Letter of Jan. 1835. *Remains*, I.

[2] *Remains*, I, pp. 434–435. The friend spoken of here is sometimes identified with Keble, but as Froude's views regarding the Reformation seem to have taken shape during the years when he was intimate with Newman, and his first expression of them is in a letter to Newman of Jan. 1832, it seems impossible to apply the reference to Keble whom he had known intimately since 1823. On the other hand, we find Keble at a later period echoing Froude's view. " As to the Reformers," he writes to his sister in Nov. 1838, " I certainly do think that as a set they belonged to the same class with the Puritans and Radicals, and I have very little doubt that if we had lived in those times, neither my father, nor you, nor Prevost, nor Harrison, would have had anything to do with them. And I think we shall never be able to make our ground good against either Romanists or Puritans till we have separated ourselves and our Liturgy from them."

me such snubs for speaking disrespectfully of them that
I did not recover them for a week or a fortnight. He
was a long time giving up Cranmer."

Froude's alienation from the Reformation was
accompanied by a growing admiration for the mediæval
Church. St. Thomas of Canterbury and the great
mediæval popes, above all Gregory VII., were to him
what St. Athanasius and the Greek Fathers were to
Newman. He admired in mediæval Catholicism the
very things that rendered it obnoxious to the Protestant
mind—its theocratic claims, its faith in the Real
Presence, its devotion to Our Lady and to the saints,
and its exaltation of asceticism and voluntary chastity.
In all this he went far beyond Newman, who was
never a mediævalist, and who at this time still retained
his traditional Protestant prejudices, regarding the
Papal claims as anti-Christian and the worship of the
saints as idolatrous. It may well be doubted if Newman
would ever have freed himself from the deep-seated
influence of these ideas, if it had not been for the
constant pressure of Froude's objections and criticisms.
He could not dismiss the ideas of his beloved Froude
with the moral indignation or the intellectual contempt with which he would have treated them if they
had come from a stranger. And so the barbed darts
of Froude's paradoxes and questionings penetrated
the surface of his consciousness and prevented him
from resting secure, like other men, in the shelter of his
inherited prejudices, even when Froude's living voice
was silenced by death.

Signs of this process are to be found in those imaginary
conversations, held at Rome in 1833, which were finally

published in the *British Magazine* in 1836 under the title " Home Thoughts from Abroad." Whether Newman intended it or not, it is impossible not to recognize the views of Froude, and sometimes his very voice and personality, in the anonymous friend of the author who puts the case for Rome against Newman's ideal of the Anglican *Via Media*.[1] The latter, he argues, is nothing but a theory which has slept in libraries, while the actual Church of England has ranked itself with the Protestants. Moreover, it contradicts the principle of development, since it implies its appeal to antiquity, a return to the unformed state in which the Church existed before Constantine. It is a substitution of infancy for manhood. Rome, on the other hand, is a reality, it is the centre of Catholic unity from which we have severed ourselves, and though we may say that the Catholic body is corrupt, can we hope that the amputated limb will be in a healthier condition by itself? In any case there cannot be two Catholic bodies, it is a contradiction in terms, and if we ask which is Catholic, Rome can appeal to precisely the same principle which St. Augustine invoked against the Donatists and St. Cyril against heretics in general. The Catholic Church

[1] It is true that he speaks of him as though he was not a very intimate friend and as one whose ideas he disapproved of. But all his characteristics, his paradoxical opinions, his profession of the principle of " bigotry " against the fashionable views of the day, his random way of talking, his ardent temperament, and his attractive character all suggest Froude, apart from the fact that he so often voices Froude's own opinions and arguments. And it is natural enough that Newman should not wish to identify Froude too closely with views of which he himself disapproved. The paper was apparently written in 1835, and consequently may reflect the influence of his later discussions and arguments with Froude in that year rather than the earlier period at which the dialogue is supposed to have taken place.

is the Church that is everywhere called Catholic, even by its enemies and those in schism from it. " Now I am only contending," he goes on, " for the *fact* that the communion of Rome constitutes the main body of the Church Catholic, and that we are split off from it, and in the condition of the Donatists ; so that every merit of Augustine's argument to them could be applied to us. This, I say, is a *fact ;* and if it be a grave fact, to account for it by saying they are corrupt is only bringing in a second grave fact. Two such serious facts—that we are separate from the great body of the Church, and that it is corrupt—should, one would think, make us serious ; whereas we behave as if they were plus and minus, and destroyed each other. Or rather we *triumph* in the Romanists being corrupt, and we *deny* they are the great body of Christians, unfairly merging their myriad of churches under the poor title of ' *the* Church of Rome ' ; as if unanimity destroyed the argument from numbers." [1]

To all this Newman has a perfectly simple answer. Truth is preferable to unity, and it is better that the Church itself should perish, if that were possible, rather than the Truth should fail, for even the Church is a means to an end—the gospel of Truth. Rome is in error, because it practises idolatry. Therefore it is our duty to separate ourselves from Rome. We have a better unity than that of external communion, the unity of true faith that unites us with the Church of the Fathers and with the Anglican divines of the great age.

It is remarkable to see how in this dialogue Newman already states so clearly the arguments that were at a

[1] *British Magazine,* IX. *Discussions and Arguments,* pp. 4–8.

later period to appeal to him with irresistible force, but by which at that time he was entirely unconvinced. There can, I think, be no doubt that they first came to him through the medium of Froude's mind, possibly at Rome itself, since we know from Froude's letters that he was interested at this time in the problem of reunion, and even went so far as to visit Wiseman at the English College, together with Newman, in order to discuss the subject.[1]

Actually, however, Froude's Catholic sympathies were not increased by his experiences in Italy. Sicily, the first Catholic country that he visited, was of all Catholic Europe the furthest from his ideal of what a Catholic country should be. He found a Church that submitted as tamely to the exploitation of the State as the Church in England, and a people that seemed "to hold the truth in unrighteousness," living in a practical paganism that was all the more shocking for their external religiosity. It was a state of things which showed all the vices and squalor of the Middle Ages without their theocratic and ascetic ideals. Above all, the travellers were appalled by the poverty and misery of the common people. "I never knew what human suffering was before," writes Newman, "children and youths who look as if they did not know what fresh air was, though they had it in plenty—well, what water

---

[1] *Remains*, I, pp. 306–308. This visit made a deep impression on Cardinal Wiseman's mind. Twenty years afterwards he wrote : " It remains marked with gratitude in my mind as an epoch in my life." " From that hour I watched with intense interest and love the Movement of which I then caught the first glimpse. My studies changed their course, the bent of my mind was altered, in the strong desire to co-operate in the new mercies of Providence." *Essays on Various Subjects*, II, p. 93.

was—with features sunk, contracted with perpetual dirt as if dirt was their food. The towns of Partenico and Alcamo are masses of filth ; the street is a pool ; but Calatafimi, where we slept !—I dare not mention facts. Suffice it to say, we found the poor children of the house slept in holes dug into the wall, which smelt, not like a dog-kennel, but like a wild beast's cage, almost overpowering us in the room upstairs." [1]

The conclusion that both Froude and Newman drew from what they saw was that " the whole western world was tending to some dreadful crisis," [2] that " the whole Christian system all over Europe ' *tendit visibiliter ad non esse.*' " [3] " I am impressed with a sad presentiment," says Newman, " as if the gift of truth when once lost was lost for ever. And so the Christian world is gradually becoming barren and effete, as land which has been worked out and has become sand. We have lasted longer than the south, but we too are going, as it would seem." [4]

The same idea of an inevitable process of decay inspires one of the many sonnets that Newman composed at this time :—

> Now is the Autumn of the Tree of Life ;
> Its leaves are shed upon the unthankful earth,
> Which lets them whirl a prey to the winds' strife,
> Heartless to store them for the months of dearth,
> Men close the door, and dress the cheerful hearth,
> Self-trusting still ; and in his comely gear
> Of precept and of rite, a household Baal rear.
>
> But I will out amid the sleet and view
> Each shrivelling stalk and silent-falling leaf ;

[1] *Letters and Correspondence*, I, p. 309.
[2] *Ibid.*, I, p. 310.
[3] Froude's *Remains*, I, p. 296.
[4] *Letters and Correspondence*, I, p. 295 (Jan. 26, 1833).

Truth after truth, of choicest strength and hue,
Fades, and in fading stirs the Angels' grief,
Unanswered here, for she, once pattern chief
Of faith, my country, now gross hearted grown
Waits but to burn the stem before her idol's throne.[1]

So far from discouraging them, however, this sense of impending catastrophe only strengthened the fierceness of their opposition to the spirit of the age, and their determination to strike a blow for the cause before it was too late.

This apocalyptic spirit finds expression in the verses of *Lyra Apostolica* which was the product of the Mediterranean journey and which is perhaps the most remarkable literary product of the Oxford Movement, since it is not concerned with the details of ecclesiastical controversy, like the *Tracts for the Times*, but was the spontaneous expression of the state of mind which generated the movement. Froude's personal contribution to it is comparatively small. But his spirit breathes through it all and finds a clear utterance in the motto which he chose for it at Rome from the *Iliad*: "Let them know that I am back again, though I long refrained from war," or as Newman phrases it, "You shall know the difference now that I am back again." The choice is characteristic of Froude, whom his friends thought of as the young Achilles, and who might well have taken as his own that other verse: "Well do I know that it is my lot to perish, nevertheless I will in no way cease till I have given the Trojans their fill of war," since, like Achilles, Froude himself fought with the consciousness of death upon him.

[1] *Lyra Apostolica*, No. 128 ; cf. No. 138.

"The world has cycles in its course, when all
That once has been, is acted o'er again ; "

On the other hand, Newman's contribution to *Lyra Apostolica* far surpasses all the rest both in amount and in quality. It includes some of the most remarkable examples of modern English religious poetry, though it has never, I think, received the attention that its literary merits deserve. The fact is that English taste demands a sweetish flavour in religious poetry, as we see from the enormous popularity of *The Christian Year*, and it is somewhat disconcerted by the stern and sometimes harsh note of Newman's verse. Some Victorian critic has remarked that *Lyra Judaica* expresses the spirit of the work better than its present title, and there is certainly something Semitic in its fierce denunciation of the apostasy of the age and its announcement of divine judgement :—

> Bide thou thy time !
> Watch with meek eyes the race of pride and crime,
> Sit in the gate and be the heathens jest,
> Smiling and self-possest.
> O thou, to whom is pledged a victors sway
> Bide thou the victor's day !

> * * * * * *

> Such need is gain
> Wait the bright Advent that shall lose thy chain !
> E'en now the shadows break, and gleams divine
> Edge the dim distant line,
> When thrones are trembling, and earth's fat ones quail,
> True Seed ! thou shalt prevail ! [1]

So may the captives of Israel have waited for the Day of the Lord in Nineveh and Babylon, but it is hardly the attitude that one would expect to find in a contemporary of Macaulay and Sydney Smith. Nevertheless it is the true stuff of poetry, if poetry be as Keble

---

[1] No. 166, " The Afflicted Church."

taught, the controlled expression of intense feeling and conviction :—

> Prune thou thy words, the thoughts control
>   That o'er thee swell and throng,
> They will condense within thy soul
>   And change to purpose strong.

writes Newman, and there is a classical severity and restraint in all his work which distinguishes it from the looser and more facile verse of Keble and Isaac Williams. But there is more in Newman's poetry than the *sæva indignatio* that inspires his attack on Liberalism. " Out of the strong comes forth sweetness," and there is a tenderness and depth of feeling in some of Newman's verse that is unsurpassed in English religious poetry. This is already to be seen in the poem that he wrote on his sister's death, years before 1833, and in *Lyra Apostolica* itself in the beautiful verses that deal with death and the state of the faithful departed—" Rest " and " Separation." The severe restraint of Newman's religious verse was indeed closely linked with an intense sensitiveness to personal relations, as we see in the verse which recalls his parting from Froude in 1832,[1] and above all in the concluding lines which he added to " Separation " on Froude's death in 1836 :—

---

[1] " It was when the cholera was imminent we parted as if, perhaps, we might not see each other again. With reference to the memory of that parting, when I shook hands with him and looked into his face with great affection I afterwards wrote the stanza :

> And when thine eye surveys
> With fond adoring gaze,
> And yearning heart, thy friend,
> Love to its grave doth tend."

Letters, I, p. 240.

> Dearest ! he longs to speak as I to know,
>   And yet we both refrain :
> It were not good ; a little doubt below
>   And all will soon be plain.

No less than eighty-five of these poems were composed during the Mediterranean journey itself, and they bear witness to the remarkable release of creative energy that took place during this vital phase of his development. His close intercourse with Froude, his intense brooding over the misfortunes of the Church and the apostasy of the age combined with the new sights and impressions of the Mediterranean world to stimulate his mind and arouse its sleeping powers. He was intoxicated by the splendour of the mountains and the sea, by the memories of the classical past and by the grandeur of Christian Rome. He was at once attracted and repelled by the spectacle of a Christianity so unlike that which he had known. In comparison with the sobriety of Anglican worship, the highly coloured piety of the Catholic south struck him as half pagan and half Methodist.[1] Yet it impressed him in spite of himself.[2] Above all, throughout his journey he was overwhelmed by a growing sense of his personal mission—of a divine power setting him apart for some high purpose and leading him he knew not where. It runs through all the poems of *Lyra*

---

[1] " It is Sunday morning. I think of St. Mary's and Littlemore. We do not know how great our privileges are. All the quiet and calm connected with our services is so beautiful in memory, and so soothing, after the sight of that most exciting religion which is around me— statues of the Madonna and the Saints in the streets, etc., etc.—a more poetical but not less jading stimulus than a pouring forth in a Baptist chapel ! " Newman to his Mother, Jan. 27, 1833. *Letters and Correspondence*, I, p. 297.

[2] Cf. " The Good Samaritan," quoted at the head of this chapter.

Apostolica from the lines " Are these the tracks of some unearthly Friend," which he wrote at Whitchurch as he waited to catch the Falmouth mail on the eve of his departure, to "Lead kindly Light," which was composed in the Straits of St. Bonifacio as he returned. Perhaps its most characteristic expression is to be found in the noble sonnet "Melchizedek," which I have already quoted, where Newman sees the traces of a divine purpose in that sense of spiritual loneliness and expatriation that haunted him throughout his life.

Newman was profoundly conscious of the heavy price that the prophetic vocation entails. Standing on the threshold of his seven-years' period of success and fame, he already had a premonition of disappointment and failure, which he expresses in the almost prophetic verses entitled " Heavenly Leadings " :—

> Did we but see,
> When life first opened how our journey lay
> Between its earliest and its closing day ;
> Or view ourselves as we sometime shall be
> Who strive for the high prize, such sight would break
> The youthful spirit, though bold for Jesus sake.
>
> But Thou, dear Lord !
> While I traced out bright scenes that were to come,
> Isaac's pure blessings, and a verdant home,
> Didst spare me, and withhold Thy fearful word ;
> Wiling me year by year, till I am found
> A pilgrim pale, with Paul's sad girdle bound."

This sense of divine fatality—of *predestination*—reached its climax in the weeks of fever and loneliness that he spent in Sicily after he had left the Froudes. " When I went down to Sicily by myself," he wrote to Keble, years afterwards, " I had a strong idea that God was going to effect some purpose by me. And from Rome I wrote to someone, I think Christie, saying I thought I was to be made something of in His Hands, 'though if not, the happier for me.' And when I was in Sicily by myself, it seemed as if someone were battling against me, and the idea has long been in my mind, though I cannot say when it came on, that my enemy was then attempting to destroy me." [1]

This obscure conflict with the forces of disease and the powers of darkness, in a strange land, set an indelible mark on Newman's mind and finally sealed him for his mission. It was the temptation in the wilderness that preceded the public ministry. When Newman came back out of Sicily, he came like a man reborn, with all his powers released and with such exuberant confidence and energy that his friends at Oxford actually failed to recognize him. All his doubts and hesitations were left behind. The shy and sensitive young don had become a leader of men who plunged into the fray with that " mixture of fierceness and sport " which had hitherto been peculiar to Froude. " ' We'll do them,' he says at least twenty times a day," writes James Mozley, " meaning by ' them ' the present race of aristocrats and the Liberal oppressors of the Church in general." [2] But while Froude fought with the gaiety of a cavalier, Newman still preserved the sombre earnestness of the Puritan tradition. When a friend of Liberal and Evangelical views wrote to remonstrate with him on the line he was taking, he answered in true covenanting style : " We will ride over you and yours, as Othniel prevailed over Cushan-

---

[1] *Correspondence with John Keble and Others* (1917), p. 315.
[2] *Letters of J. B. Mozley*, p. 36.

Rishathaim, King of Mesopotamia." [1]   As Newman himself remarks, this fierceness inevitably aroused hostility and opposition.   Nevertheless we may question whether the Oxford Movement would have gone far without it, for hatred and love are but two aspects of the same thing, and the love that knows no hatred is but the ghost of love.   That is why the mild and gentle Keble taught his disciples the duty of hatred— if they would be true lovers, they must learn how to hate.   To-day, no doubt, we have learned better.   But if religion no longer arouses passion, it is because our minds are no longer alive to religious issues.   When life still flows strong in economics and politics, there is no lack of hatred, and hatred that has no spiritual principle to restrain it from evil.   It is since religion has gone out of European life that the era of proscriptions and persecution has returned.   Hence we have little excuse for assuming an attitude of moral superiority towards the past.   If Newman and Keble and Froude were severe against opinions, they were singularly gentle in their treatment of individuals.   Few men vilified the leaders of the Oxford Movement more bitterly than Arnold and Whately—one referred to them as the Oxford Malignants, and the other as " thugs "— yet Newman throughout his career continued to speak of them not merely politely, but even with affection. And Froude and Keble were equally free from ill will and rancour.   For all their fierceness the leaders of the Oxford Movement were loyal and chivalrous fighters.

[1] This appears to refer to the letter printed by Frank Newman in his *Contributions to the Early History of the late Cardinal Newman*.   If so, it is a much milder affair than one would suppose from Newman's own account of it.

V. *APOSTOLICALS AND CONSERVATIVES*

CONSERVATISM

How long, O Lord of grace,
Must languish Thy true race,
In a fixed friendship linked with Belial here ;
With Mammon's brand of care,
And Baal pleading fair,
And the dog-breed who at Thy Temple jeer ?

How long, O Lord, how long
Shall Cæsar do us wrong,
Laid but as steps to throne his mortal power ?
While e'en our Angels stand
With helpless voice and hand,
Scorned by proud Haman, in his triumph-hour.

'Tis said our seers discern
The destined bickerings stern,
In the dim distance, of Thy fiery train.
O nerve us in that woe !
For, where Thy wheels shall go,
We must be tried, the while Thy foes are shain.

J. H. N.

(These verses from the *Lyra* are used by Hurrell Froude as the Envoy
of his long essay on " State Interference in Matters Spiritual.")

THE Mediterranean journey had no less importance
for the development of Froude's ideas than for that of
Newman's, though in a different way. For while it
led Newman into the wilderness to wrestle with the
spirit, it brought Froude for the first time into contact
with the new currents of European thought. Anglican
writers for the most part tend to minimize the influence
of the continental Catholic revival on the Oxford
Movement, and no doubt they are justified with regard
to the main High Church tradition which was essen-

tially English. But with Froude the case is different. In this, as in other matters, he was far from being a typical Anglican, and the ideas which he derived from the contemporary ultramontane movement in France had a very important influence on his own thought and, through him, on the development of the Oxford Movement.

While Newman was lying sick in Sicily, Froude was returning through France, in order to visit the places connected with St. Thomas's exile. There he came to hear of the religious movement which was taking place in France under the leadership of Lamennais, and he suddenly became aware that the same problems that occupied his mind were being discussed with passionate earnestness by Catholics on the Continent. In France the same struggle between Liberalism and Traditionalism was being fought out, but on a wider field and with more imposing forces. There the enemy was not the watered-down Liberalism of the English reformers and their Whig allies, but the party of revolution who marched under the banner of Voltaire and Rousseau, while the cause of religion was championed not by a shy and diffident scholar, like Keble, who kept aloof from the world in the retirement of a county parsonage, but by a man of genius who had descended into the arena and fought with all the weapons of the journalist and the popular agitator. Lamennais had wider and more ambitious dreams than any of the leaders of the Oxford Movement. He believed that the new social order that was arising in Europe demanded a spiritual principle and that it could only find this principle in Catholicism. " The world has changed," he wrote, " it seeks a master ; it is orphaned, it seeks a father." To attempt to stop the march of change was to fight against God who was leading the world by new paths. " Go back or stop, men cannot if they would. An irresistible power forces them ever onwards. What matters, the perils and the fatigues of their march ? They say like the Crusaders : ' God wills it.' " [1] If the Church were to put herself at the head of this movement, instead of offering an unintelligent and unavailing resistance to it, she would recover civilization for Christ and once more, as in the Middle Ages, become the mistress of the spirit of the age.

This attitude is of course fundamentally different from that of the leaders of the Oxford Movement. Their conservatism was as intransigent as that of the French royalists, although, unlike the latter, they believed that there was a certain natural affinity between Liberalism and Popery. Thus in his essay on Lamennais in the *British Critic* for 1837 Newman traces " a clear connexion between his theology and the popular philosophy of the day." Lamennais' belief in progress is to him the natural corollary of the Romish doctrine of development—in contrast to the Anglican belief in Antiquity, which does not admit of either development or progress.[2] Moreover, the fundamental error of Lamennais, his failure to recognize that rebellion is a sin, shows that he is " the true disciple of the Gregories and Innocents of past times." [3]

[1] " The Fall of De La Mennais " in *Essays Historical and Critical*, I, p. 159 (from *Affaires de Rome*).
[2] *Ibid.*, pp. 158–159.
[3] *Ibid.*, p. 157.

This faithfully represents what one may call the classical High Church position to which Newman, like Keble, still adhered, but it is far less representative of the views of Hurrell Froude, who was by way of being a " disciple of the Gregories and Innocents " himself. He lacked the insularity of the typical Anglican, and his mind was far more open and receptive to new ideas. Though no doubt Froude was repelled by the democratic element in Lamennais' programme and his sympathy with the revolutionary movements in Ireland and on the Continent, he was at the same time still more powerfully attracted by the ultramontane ideal of the spiritual sovereignty of the Church and its complete independence of the State, which Lamennais defended with such vigour and eloquence. Froude had already felt the alliance of the High Church party with Conservatism irksome, but the alliance was so deeply rooted in the Anglican tradition that no help could be looked for from an appeal to Hooker and Laud, whose authority merely consecrated the principle of the alliance. But Lamennais' attack on Gallicanism reached the very centre of the problem and rejected the whole system of Church establishment on the ground of first principles. Galli-canism had claimed to secure the freedom of the national Church, actually it meant something entirely different—the enslavement of the Church to the State. As Newman puts it : " That great and ancient power, the Church Catholic which dates her origin from the first preaching of the Gospel, which was founded by the Apostles, and which claims to be indissolubly connected with its fortunes, has been taken captive by

her enemies, blinded, and set to servile employments—
to make men good citizens and to promote the enlightenment and comfort of the world ; except when she is
brought out of the prison house on some great pageant,
' to make sport,' to invest the institutions of earth
with something of a religious character, and to pay
homage to its mighty men, as her creators and
governors." [1]

This was precisely what Froude felt with regard to
the Church of England. He realized that Liberalism
was not the only enemy. Even more dangerous was
the interested friendship of the party which regarded
the Church as a bulwark of the established order.
Henceforward he accepted Lamennais' view of the
relations between Church and State and denounced
the Erastianism of the Anglican establishment with
the same arguments and sometimes with the same
words with which Gallicanism was attacked in the
pages of *L'Avenir*. He no longer regarded himself as
a High Churchman—a Z, as he contemptously terms
them—he was an " Apostolical," a champion of the
Divine Right of the Church against Crown and
Parliament as well as against Liberals and Dissenters.
Though he regretted the romantic associations of the
old order, as we see in his sonnet " Farewell to Toryism,"
he realized that the Church must be separated from its
class associations and that what he calls " the gentleman
heresy " must be denounced as such. " We will have
a *vocabularium apostolicum*," he writes to Newman on
October 27 1833, " and I will start it with four words :
' pampered aristocrat,' ' resident gentlemen,' ' smug

[1] *Essays*, I, p. 138. " The Fall of De La Mennais."

parsons,' ' *pauperes Christi.*' I shall use the first on all occasions ; it seems to me just to hit the thing." [1]

This breach with " Toryism " and with the agrarian aristocratic tradition of the Established Church is the more remarkable because Froude was himself the off-spring of that tradition, and had inherited all its loyalties and prejudices. It is one of the chief features that distinguishes the nascent Tractarian movement from the old High Church party which took " Church and King " for its watchword, and it is this principle that made it possible for the Oxford Movement to attract new disciples from the opposite Liberal camp, such as W. G. Ward. But this was not the only thing which Froude owed to the example of Lamennais. All his activity during the summer of 1833 was coloured by it, and it is even possible that the idea of the Tracts themselves which, if we may believe the testimony of Isaac Williams,[2] was first suggested by Froude at Oxford before Newman's return, owed something to the influence of *L'Avenir*. Certainly that influence is very prominent in the propaganda against Erastianism and Conservative compromise which was launched by Froude in his articles in the *British Magazine* from July onwards. Those articles, which were reprinted in the *Remains*,[3] under the title " Remarks on State Interference in Matters Spiritual," form Froude's most considerable contribution to the literature of the movement and show that he possessed Lamennais' ability as an ecclesiastical controversialist and, even

---

[1] *Remains*, I, p. 329.
[2] *The Autobiography of Isaac Williams* (1892), p. 64.
[3] *Remains*, III, pp. 184–269.

more, as a political pamphleteer. It opens with a terrific attack on the undenominational principle as seen in the policy of Sir Robert Peel and the Conservatives, who were prepared to abandon the religious exclusivism of the older Toryism in order to unite all the moderate elements in the country on the side of Conservatism. "A union between excellent men of all parties for the maintenance of peace and order ; excellent, truly, and of all parties. . . . Excellent Independents ; and excellent Socinians ; and excellent Jews ; excellent aliens from the Church of Christ ; excellent unbelievers in the faith, in the which ' he that believeth not shall be damned ' ; and, to amalgamate the strange mass, excellent latitudinarians, who, like Gallio, care for none of these things. These *excellent persons* are to come together, and waiving those *minor points* on which they differ, to unite on those of which all acknowledge the importance ; *the maintenance of peace and good order.*" [1]

Before Churchmen consented to such a union in order to avoid greater evils let them consider what it involved. It meant that the Church of England was to cease to be the Church of the nation but was still to be ruled by the government of the nation, by a government that might be composed of heretics or Jews, and that would probably use its power for secular political ends. This in itself is the greatest of evils, and rather than accept it, it would be better to sacrifice wealth and influence in order to preserve the essential liberties of the Church.

In all this Froude is paraphrasing or quoting the

[1] *Remains*, III, p. 189.

pages of *L'Avenir*, and he concludes with a passage
from Lacordaire's appeal to the Bishops of France.
" QUE CRAIGNEZ VOUS ! N'ETES VOUS PAS EVEQUES ?
Bishops of Christ's holy everlasting Church : who
shall interfere with the free exercise of your indelible
prerogative ? Consecrate or refuse to consecrate : who
shall reverse your decree ? You can bind, and who
shall loose ? UNE SEULE CHOSE LEUR EST POSSIBLE ;
LE RETRANCHEMENT DE NOTRE BUDGET. *Eveques de
France ! nous ne vous en disons pas d'avantage ; c'est à
vous de voir lequel vous préférez laisser sur vos sièges en
mourant, ou un Episcopat riche et corrupteur, ou un Episcopat
pauvre et digne de vous succeder.*" [1]

" Such are the sentiments," he continues, " of a true
Conservative : a Conservative, not of names but of
things ; not of appearances, but of realities : a
Conservative that would conserve not to a latitudinarian
government trusts that were reposed in an exclusive
government, simply because it was a government and
is a government, but to the representatives of the
Church, rights which have always belonged to the
Church, though they were once a ruling party, and are
now a persecuted party." [2]

In the following section Froude proceeds to show
that the old basis of the Anglican Establishment, as
represented by Hooker, had been destroyed by the
repeal of the Test and Corporation Act which, in fact,
amounted to the cancellation of the conditions on which
parliamentary interference in matters spiritual had

[1] This passage may, it seems to me, have inspired Newman's reference
to the English bishops in the first *Tract for the Times*.
[2] *Remains*, III, pp. 194–195.

been permissible. Nevertheless Froude does not regard the Tudor settlement itself as really justifiable. It is the result of a long series of systematic aggressions on the part of the secular power against the Church of Christ, that begins with the anti-papal legislation of the 14th century and culminates in the spoliation of the Church by Henry VIII. The State defended these aggressions under the pretext that they were resisting the usurpations of the papal power. But "however unjust and oppressive may have been the encroachments made on the independence of different national churches by the policy of the Roman pontiff, still it does not appear that the Church as such had effected any material aggression on the Rights of Christian States. Indeed, if we compare the claims of Gregory VII and his austere successors with those which Gibbon allows to have been conceded by Constantine and other Emperors to the Patriarchs of the primitive Church, it may be thought on the whole that their policy with respect to Civil Governments was directed rather to recovering losses than extending conquests." For of a truth "it was to other hands than those of Nero or Domitian that Christ had committed the precious gift, the right of choosing successors to the Apostles." It is in this that the primitive constitution of the Church consists. (1) "The whole body of Christ's Church asserted and maintained to themselves the right of freely choosing those who were to be their Spiritual Rulers. This right they did not think fit to make over either to the Emperor's ministers or to the Emperor himself. It was their own ; it had been bequeathed to them by the Apostles ; and they would not sell the inheritance of their fathers. (2) The persons so elected . . . deemed it in no wise incumbent on them or consistent with their duty, to consult their civil governors as to the manner in which they should administer (their office). The sword of the Holy Spirit was in their hands, and they turned it against whomsoever that Spirit pleased." [1]

In the later middle ages, however, their high apostolical principles had become obscured. " The inherent strength of the Church had been lost with its primitive constitution, and the great body of Christ's flock looked on as unconcerned spectators, amidst the selfish struggles of the Civil and Ecclesiastical powers." . . . " The wealth of bishoprics and dignities, which was once regarded as the patrimony of the poor, had by degrees assumed the character of worldly property, was bestowed by patronage, and used for selfish gratification ; while the lordly personages who possessed it, with the enjoyment of riches had imbibed the dread of poverty, and shrunk from asserting their station as successors of the Apostles for fear of losing their station in society.

In this melancholy and fallen condition that edifice against which the gates of Hell shall not finally prevail, became a ready prey to the rapacious Henry. It had been polluted, it fell ;—shall it ever rise again ? " [2]

According to Froude's view the one remedy for the situation was a return to the Apostolical principle of authority and a reassertion of the inherent rights of the Church, not of the Church of England by law estab-

[1] *Remains*, III, pp. 219–220.
[2] *Ibid.*, p. 227.

lished, which was the only object of conservative solicitude, but of " the congregations of Christ's little ones, the poor, the halt, the lame and the blind." How could this be done in face of the Act of Supremacy and all the statutes of the Reformation settlement? Froude's solution was a simple and ingenious one : to go behind the Reformation and cut out the original root of the evil by a repeal of *Præmunire*. For since the whole force of the Act of 20 Henry VIII resided in the application of the penalties of *Præmunire* to those who refused to elect the royal nominee to a vacant see, the repeal of *Præmunire* would draw the fangs of the later legislation and make free canonical election of bishops once more possible. Actually Froude could not have chosen better ground on which to fight : for the Anglican system of the appointment of bishops with its *congé d'élire* and letters mandatory is a glaring example of the legal anomalies which the Reform Parliament was pledged to sweep away. What could be more absurd than to demand that men should " maturely and seriously consider concerning a fit person to be elected," and then to threaten them with the extreme penalties of outlawry and forfeiture if they exercised their discretion by refusing to elect the government's nominee ?

Accordingly Froude was able to turn the tables neatly on the party of comprehension by appealing to dissenters and to all men of good will to join in a " union of excellent men of all parties " for the removal of a flagrant injustice. " Surely it is not unreasonable to call on our dissenting countrymen to join in effecting the speedy removal of a grievance such as this, so much more severer than any which themselves have experienced. This is no question for party jealousy ; it involves no doctrined nicety, no principle of politics : it turns not on the peculiarities of sect or faction ; Presbyterian, Quaker, Independent, Socinians, all must agree on it, all, in short, whose creed obliges them to uprightness and fair dealing, who profess to act on the broad principles of common sense and common honesty." [1]

This practical measure was but the spearhead of Froude's wider programme which aimed at a thoroughgoing restoration of spiritual autonomy and apostolic discipline. He believed that the day of national churches was over, and that the attempt to preserve the outward form of one was destructive of the inner substance. " The true cause of the decay of Church Discipline," he wrote in the following year, " is not that nations have become Christian, but that the clergy wished them to appear Christian, either before they were so or after they ceased to be so. And if at the present day it is difficult to enforce Church Discipline in England, it is not because we have a national church, but because the clergy are too anxious to keep up the show of one.

The body of the English nation either are sincere Christians, or they are not ; if they are, they will submit to Discipline as readily as the primitive Christians did ; if not, let us tell the truth and shame the devil : let us give up a *national* Church and have a *real* one." [2]

I have dealt at such length with Froude's papers on

---

[1] *Ibid.*, p. 257.
[2] *Remains*, III, p. 274. " Remarks on Church Discipline."

Church Reform, not only because they are so little known even to those who are familiar with the general history of the Oxford Movement, but also because they show better perhaps than anything else the quality of Froude's mind and the vigour and clarity of his thought. He is regarded by some writers as a morbidly introspective pietist, by others as a witty and irresponsible young man who enjoyed shocking people with his paradoxes. In reality he was a natural leader of men and a born fighter who possessed, as J. B. Mozley remarks, great practical and almost lawyer-like penetration. He had none of the English genius for compromise or the Anglican faculty of shutting the eyes to unpleasant facts. With him it was all or nothing, and like the Homeric Ajax he was prepared to face defeat so long as he was not compelled to fight in the dark.

This love of clear thought and drastic action explains his sympathy and understanding for the ideas of the Neo-Ultramontane school. Indeed, he would have been more at home in the clear air of Catholic Paris than among the misty half-lights and changing shadows of Anglican Oxford. There is something pathetic in the spectacle of Froude's gallant attempt to transform the whole constitution and ethos of the Anglican Church with no allies besides a scholarly recluse like Keble and two or three young dons. Nevertheless, with a characteristically chivalrous contempt for odds, he set himself to carry out a programme which was equally obnoxious to Liberal politicians and Conservative churchmen. Nor can his attempt be regarded as an entire failure, since, though he failed to carry the Oxford Movement with him as a whole, he infused a great deal of his spirit into its two great leaders, Newman and Keble. " Keble is my fire," he wrote, " but I may be his poker." And, in fact, there can be little doubt that the transformation of the gentle pietism of *The Christian Year* into the apocalyptic earnestness of the Keble of the Assize sermon was largely Froude's work. All Keble's finest contributions to *Lyra Apostolica*—and they are certainly superior in quality to the poems of *The Christian Year*— " The Watch by Night," " Christian Chivalry " and " Church and King " bear the mark of Froude's spirit— his crusading idealism and his high contempt for expediency and compromise, and the same is true, as we have already noted, with regard to Newman's more powerful genius.

At the moment, however, when Froude began to organize his campaign for the Apostical cause against Erastianism and Liberalism, neither Keble nor Newman were present in Oxford, and he was forced to fall back on Isaac Williams, the mildest of the mild, and the ponderous William Palmer.[1]

The first step—the historic beginning of the Oxford Movement in the strict sense—was taken at the close of the summer term in a conversation with Isaac Williams in the garden of Trinity College. The latter has recorded it in two versions, one in prose in his auto-biography and the other in some of the flattest verses that are to be found in English literature. In this version Froude's concluding speech runs as follows :

[1] William Palmer, of Trinity College, Dublin, and Worcester College, Oxford (1803–1885), a very different person from that attractive and original figure William Palmer, of Magdalen.

                              " My friend
You now must creep no more ; for all too long
You have in country hamlets shady grown.
For part of this our duty, ere we die,
Is to be up and stirring ; we must rise
Or be for ever fallen : God will help
Else all that's good and holy in the land,
Beneath the blasting influence of the State
Will wither and dry up and droop and die,
As 'neath the upas-tree. We must be up,
And moving, now, at once ; and when our friend
Shall have returned from ancient Sicily,"
(He spake of one whom he had left behind
Bound for the classic shores of Syracuse),
" Tracts we must have, and, by what means we can,
Launch them abroad, short Tracts ; we must begin,
And you, too, you must aid, and with your verse.
Come, see what you have ready for our hand.
The *Monthly*, as you know, *The British* named,
Is open for our letters, prose, and rhyme.
But deeper the foundations must be laid
In these our Tracts ; subsidial aid we need,
Full many : to get friends (if here and there
One may be found, or two) to bring to aid
Their pulpits, and proclaim there is a Church
Planted by Christ's own hand within our isle.—
And let us now to Worcester." Then of one
He spake, well-honoured for good service done
Linking our Liturgies unto the past.
" Hearty he is, and earnest ; though not meet
Throughout to understand and sympathise,
Yet in his line will lend us his good aid,
Though looking for external front, and powers,
More than on principles which we are bent
To scatter wide and deep. Let's now to him."
And thus, full-sailed in academic garb,
Through the Collegiate gates, archway, and porch
We passed in conversation, bent to raise
The Signal : 'twas the day of little things.[1]

What Froude actually said was short and to the
point, like all his conversation. " Isaac, we must
make a row in the world. Why shouldn't we ? . . .
Newman and I are determined to set to work as soon
as he returns and you must join us. We must have
short tracts, and letters in the *British Magazine* and

[1] From " The Origin of the Tracts for the Times," in *Thoughts in Past Years*, 6th ed., 1852, pp. 323-4.

verses, and get people to preach sermons on the
Apostolical succession and the like. And let us come
and see old Palmer and get him to do something." [1]
Froude's first allies were singularly ill-chosen. Poor
Isaac Williams was no more capable of " making a row
in the world " than a highly conscientious sheep,
though he was deeply attached to both Keble and
Froude.[2] Palmer, on the other hand, was in every
respect the antithesis of Froude, a man of more learning
than imagination, pompous, long-winded and with no
sense of humour : a strong High Churchman, who
retained the Irish Protestant's horror of Popery ; a
thorough Conservative, who desired above all things to
preserve the union of the Church with the State, and
who had a " certain connexion in the Establishment,
consisting of high Church dignitaries, Archdeacons,
London rectors and the like, who belonged to what
was commonly called the high-and-dry school." [3]   In

[1] Williams' *Autobiography*, p. 63.

[2] The passage which I have already quoted from Isaac Williams'
Thoughts in Past Years, concludes with a not unworthy tribute to his dead
friend.

> That friend with whom I thus in council walked,
> Associate of my earlier years long since
> Is in his peaceful grave ; nor did he live
> To see our sorrows.   There was that in him
> Where in one might cast anchor.

> *   *   *   *   *

> One by himself, not of a class or kind,
> Like to himself alone and no one else.
> There was within him such repose or Truth,
> Absence of self, such heart-controlling fear,
> I feel that had he lived he had not been
> The sport of his own sails, or popular winds
> That he had courted for our object's sake.
> Men hurry to and fro ; but he the while
> Hath found the Haven where he fain would be.

[3] Newman, *Apologia* (ed. cit.), pp. 142-143.

short, he was what Froude would call " a regular Z," and it is difficult to understand how they could ever have found anything in common with one another. Probably Froude's vehement anti-Liberalism blinded Palmer to the essential radicalism of his views, while Palmer's readiness to engage in an active campaign against the ecclesiastical policy of the Government led Froude to overlook his essential Conservatism. For Palmer, after all, supplied an invaluable link between Oxford and the High Church movement in the rest of England.

Above all, he was in close touch with Hugh James Rose,[1] the great grandson of Alexander Rose, the nonjuror, and who was at this time undoubtedly the leading representative of High Church opinion in the country. It was he who had inaugurated the Anglican revival by the foundation of the *British Magazine*, in 1832, as the official organ of the High Church party, and who, as Newman wrote in the dedication of the fourth volume of his sermons, " when hearts were failing bade us stir up the gift that was in us, and betake ourselves to our true mother." Froude was particularly anxious to enlist Rose in the Apostolical cause, and perhaps hoped that the *British Magazine* might become the *Avenir* of the new movement. If so, his hopes were doomed to disappointment. The famous conference at Rose's rectory at Hadleigh from July 18 to 25, attended by Froude, Palmer, and the Hon. A. P. Perceval, proved an almost complete fiasco. Each of

[1] Born 1795, Fellow of Trinity College, Cambridge, Rector of Hadleigh, Principal of King's College, London, 1836, died at Florence, 1838.

the participants was intent on carrying his own particular project, Palmer wanted a national Association of Friends of the Church with rules and meetings and a committee of " safe, sound, sensible men " like Joshua Watson, and Norris ; Rose insisted that everything should be done through the *British Magazine*, while Perceval's pet scheme was the promulgation of a " Churchman's Manual," which would form a kind of compendium of High Church doctrine. All of them, except perhaps Perceval, united to scout Froude's revolutionary plans for the repeal of *Præmunire* and the return to the Apostolical constitution of the Church. Although both Palmer and Perceval afterwards published their accounts of the meeting, we have no detailed record of Froude's part in it. We can, however, form some idea of it from Lord Blachford account of a similar encounter between Froude and Palmer some time in the same year. " I remember," he says, " one day his grievously shocking Palmer of Worcester, a man of an opposite texture, when a council in J. H. N.'s rooms had been called to consider some memorial or other to which Palmer wanted to collect the signatures of many and particularly of dignified persons, but in which Froude wished to express the determined opinions of a few. Froude stretched out his long length on Newman's sofa and broke in upon one of Palmer's judicious harangues about Bishops and Archdeacons and such like, with the ejaculation : " I don't see why we should disguise from ourselves that our object is to dictate to the clergy of this country and I for one do not want anyone else to get on the box ! " [1]

---

[1] *The Oxford Movement*, p. 54, by R. W. Church.

We can hardly be surprised that Rose and Palmer found him a rash and impracticable young man,[1] and poor Froude had to admit his defeat in letters which in spite of their humour show that the disappointment was a bitter one. " [Rose] and [Palmer]," he wrote, " seem fully impressed with the notion that people will ' Oh ! oh ! ' any scheme for reform on High Church principle : the High Church because they are asleep, and the others, because they are so confident of their strength as to think us not worth arguing with. So they think little about my movement for the appointment of the Bishops, or any of my speculations, and, in fact, have floored me. It seems to be agreed among the wise that we must begin by laying a foundation. . . . This is a humiliating conclusion to me, and I should think a flat one to all." [2]

Keble seems to have been equally discouraged, though he was inclined to discount Froude's pessimism. On Aug. 8 he wrote to Newman : " As concerning Mater Ecclesia, I think that if the Hadleighans could not agree, where *inter quatuor muros*, will you find six men to agree together ? But I quite agree with you that Rose's magazine must be supported—unless he actually rats, which I will never believe unless I see it. As for Hurrell, he is so annoyed just now at his project not being accepted, that I count his dissatisfaction for very little." [3]

At the same time, Keble agreed with Froude in his attitude towards the State. He believed that it was

---

[1] Palmer, it is true, was the same age, but he was the type that is born old.
[2] *Remains*, I, p. 321 (letter of Aug. 14 to Henry Wilberforce).
[3] Newman, *Letters and Correspondence*, I, pp. 388–389.

far better to sacrifice the endowments of the Church rather than to acquiesce in the Church policy of the Government. " Take every pound, shilling and penny and the curse of sacrilege along with it ; only let us make our own Bishops and be governed by our own laws. This is the length I am prepared to go ; but, of course, if we could get our liberty at an easier price, so much the better," he writes to Newman. Consequently he refused to join in the protest against the separation of Church and State which Palmer and Newman had inserted in the articles that they had drawn up for the Association of Friends of the Church on the ground that " the union of Church and State in its existing form was actually sinful." [1] He even felt that it was no longer possible for him to take the oath of supremacy or to accept any further curacy or office in the Church of England.[2]

Newman, however, was not prepared to allow the incipient movement to be wrecked by premature intransigence. He alone possessed the diplomatic ability and the gift of entering into other men's minds which is necessary for party leadership, and from this moment he intervenes decisively to take command of the movement at Oxford. With regard to the Hadleigh conference, he adopted a surprisingly moderate attitude, and we find him writing to Keble on Aug. 5, urging him not to allow a break with Rose and Palmer and disavowing Froude's " violent " opinions. " Froude wishes us to break with Rose, which must

[1] Perceval, *Collection of Papers dealing with the Theological Movement of 1833* (1842), p. 12.
[2] Newman, *Letters and Correspondence*, I, pp. 388–389.

not be, I think. Let us wait the course of events. Rose is hoping for a reaction, till we clearly see it to be impossible, there is no reason we should talk of the repeal of the *Præmunire*—to say nothing of people not being prepared for it—and yet we may protest against measures we think unchristian. . . . Do you not think we should act in concert as nearly in the way of a society as possible ? *i.e.*, to take measures for the circulation of tracts, pamphlets, etc., and to write systematically to stir up our friends. . . . I fear they did not get on very well at Hadleigh. Froude wants you to give your friend Arthur Perceval a bit of advice, which I think Froude himself partly requires. We shall lose all our influence when times are worse, if we are prematurely violent. I heartily wish things may keep quiet for a year or two that we may ascertain our position, get up precedents, and know our duty. Palmer thinks both Froude and Perceval very deficient in learning, therefore rash." [1]

Froude, on his part, was ready enough to accept Newman's leadership. He recognized the latter's superior genius as a writer and a propagandist, and was quite prepared to take a back seat : *me oportet minui*. Moreover, the progress of his illness made it impossible for him to take an active part in the movement. He returned to his home in Devonshire in August, and after a brief visit to Oxford in October, he finally left England in November for the West Indies, where he was to remain until 1835. Nevertheless, his thoughts were always at Oxford, and he was continually writing to his friends, urging them to greater activity and scolding

[1] *Ibid.*, I, pp. 386–387.

them whenever he thought that they showed signs of temporizing or yielding to Palmer and the " Z.'s." As Newman, or his editress, remarks, " His more intimate friends required his criticisms and rested on his judgement. . . . Keble, in his own simple way, sends his papers to his old pupil to be overlooked by him, and Mr. Newman was more at ease with Froude's imprimatur. Thus he sends him draughts of papers ; for example : " No. 2, Keble," " No. 1, mine," with the order, " criticize the whole very accurately in matter and style and send it back by return of post." [1] It is impossible to exaggerate the importance of this collaboration, especially during the autumn of 1833, and in the production of the earlier *Tracts for The Times*. The voice may be Newman's or Keble's or Bowden's, but the spirit is the spirit of Froude, and the flame of his selfless enthusiasm burned no less brightly for being transmitted through other minds. Other men contributed their talents to the common cause, but Froude gave his whole self, and that cause owed no less to his devotion than to Newman's genius, to Pusey's learning, to the loyalty and piety of Keble.

---

[1] Newman, *Letters and Correspondence*, I, 423.

VI. *OXFORD AND THE "TRACTS FOR THE TIMES"*

OXFORD

(From Bagley at 8 a.m.)

The flood is round thee, but thy towers as yet
Are safe, and clear as by a summer's sea
Pierce the calm morning mist, serene and free,
To point in silence Heavenward. There are met
Thy foster-children ; there in order set
Their nursing fathers, sworn to Heaven and thee
(An oath renewed this hour on bended knee,)
Ne'er to betray their Mother or forget.—
Lo ! on the top of each aërial spire
What seems a star by day, so high and bright
It quivers from afar in golden light :
But 'tis a form of earth, though touched with fire
Celestial, raised in other days to tell
How, when they tired of prayer, Apostles fell.

JOHN KEBLE, April, 1833.

UP to this point the Anglican revival was still an unorganized sporadic movement which possessed no local centre of unity. Keble and Froude were indeed Oxford men, but they were neither of them in permanent residence, nor did they possess the public recognition or the semi-official status of a man like H. J. Rose. From the moment when Newman took the leadership, however, Oxford became the centre of the movement, and retained its position until Newman left the Church of England, twelve years later. This connexion does much to explain the characteristic features of the movement. A highly specialized social environment favours the development of correspondingly original types of thought and feeling, and the ethos of Tractarianism, which is so different from the utilitarian spirit of the England of the Reform Bill and the Industrial Revolution, finds its natural setting in the Oxford of the '30's which still retained its own social tradition and remained it to a great extent independent of the new economic and political forces that were beginning to dominate 19th century English culture.

We who know only the modern town which sprawls its ungainly length from industrialized Cowley to suburbanized Wolvercote can hardly realize the character of the little city which lay among its rivers and meadows, as Dean Church has described in a famous passage,[1] like an ecclesiastical community of the Middle Ages, consecrated to religion and learning (of a sort), and apart from the current of modern life· It was the sacred city of Anglicanism, into which nothing common or unclean could enter, and where neither Popery nor Dissent could obtain a foothold. Here teaching was still controlled by celibate clerical corporations, matriculation and graduation were surrounded by religious forms, and government was in the hands of a kind of gerontocracy, consisting of the heads of houses, some of whose members, like Dr. Routh, were themselves venerable relics of antiquity who linked the Oxford of Newman with the England of the Jacobites and the Nonjurors. Such a society was threatened by the liberal programme of reform not like the other orders of society merely in its abuses and privileges, but in its innermost nature and its very principle of being. Elsewhere the old order seemed to

[1] *The Oxford Movement*, pp. 139–141.

represent nothing but the vested interests of pluralists and place hunters : in Oxford it still stood for an ideal. No doubt it was an anomaly in the age of utilitarianism and industrial development. It was inefficient, cumbersome, out of date. But it was beautiful ; more beautiful perhaps than any other place in an England which was still rich in beauty : and consequently it could still inspire loyalty and affection.

Of all this Newman was conscious. He was intensely sensitive to the genius of places, and he regarded Oxford as the social embodiment of the High Church principle in the same way as Rome was the city of Catholicism and Paris the city of Liberalism and infidelity. He saw that the anti-modern character of Oxford, its unutilitarian beauty, fitted it to be the representative of religious ideals and spiritual values in an age of secularism and material progress. But he looked to Oxford for something much more than a Conservative opposition to the forces of change. He saw that it was itself capable of becoming an instrument of anti-modern change and anti-Liberal reform. If the second Reformation, of which he dreamed, could become a reality, it could only be done by capturing an organ of public opinion and organizing a centre of social influence.

Now Oxford was the great centre of Anglican theological studies and the chief school for the training of the clergy, and if it could be won over to the new principles it might become the Geneva of the second Reformation.

According to Newman's view, universities are the natural centres of intellectual movements. " Living movements," he wrote, " do not come of committees, nor are great ideas worked out through the post." They can only arise from the personal contact of living minds. The spark which Newman had caught from Froude, and Froude from Keble, must be communicated in the same way to other souls until the fire blazed out in common action.

Consequently when, five days after Newman's return from Italy, Keble preached his famous assize sermon on National Apostasy it seemed to Newman as though everything—place, time, speaker and subject —combined to mark the occasion as the starting point of the movement that he desired. Keble was not a man of action ; he had no gift for party leadership. But no one could speak with greater authority or with more intense conviction. He was the living embodiment of the High Church tradition, and principles which other men regarded as of merely historical interest were to him burning truths that ruled his whole life. While Newman and Froude had been absent in the Mediterranean, he had brooded over the Liberal attack on the Church until he felt that silence was a criminal acquiescence in an act of rebellion against God. The abolition of the Test Act and the suppression of the Irish sees seemed to him to destroy the solemn covenant between God and the English nation which was the justification of the Anglican Establishment. It was an act of National Apostasy.

This is the theme of his famous sermon. As the Chosen People had rejected the Divine Theocracy and had demanded a king to reign over them, so England " which had for centuries acknowledged as an essential part of its theory of government that as a Christian nation she was also a part of Christ's Church and bound in all her legislation and policy by the fundamental rules of that Church," was now deliberately throwing off the restraint that this principle involved and even the very principle itself and saying " we will be as the heathen, the families of the countries, the aliens to the Church of the Redeemer." [1]

Hence it was the duty of every Christian to dis-associate himself from this national crime. The revolt of the State against the divine authority did not, indeed, justify the Christian in disobeying the authority of the State. He must submit to it as to any other tyranny, but under protest and involuntarily. " This seems the least that can be done ; unless we would have our children's children say : ' There was once here a glorious Church, but it was betrayed into the hands of libertines for the real or affected love of a little temporary peace and good order.' " [2]

Like Newman, Keble had no faith in organizations and committees. But he also believed in direct action— a kind of spiritual crusade, which might unite the faith-ful few in a " glorious holy war " for the Church's cause.

> Angel of England ! who might thee withstand ?
> Who for the spoiled and trampled church deny
> Thy suit in Heavens high courts, might one true band
> Of holy brethren, breathing English air,
> Be found, their Cross in thine array to bear
> And for their Mother cast earth's dreams away ? [3]

But though Keble could preach a crusade with

---

[1] *Sermons, Academical and Occasional,* p. 134.

[2] This sentence forms the conclusion of the preface that Keble added to his sermon when preparing it for the Press a week later.

[3] *Lyra Apostolica,* CXLIX, " Church and King."

fervour and conviction, he was incapable of organizing a party or carrying on a successful propaganda. He was not a good " mixer," and though he was full of charm in the intimate society of his friends, he was apt to antagonize strangers by his brusque manners and his blunt expressions of opinions. Newman, on the other hand, had already gained a foremost position at Oxford as a preacher and theologian and possessed in addition a tact and subtlety of intelligence that made it possible for him to enter into the minds of others. Thus Newman was able to act as an intermediary between the two wings of the movement and to co-operate with Palmer and Rose without losing contact with Froude and Keble. Directly after the failure of the Hadleigh Conference he set himself to organize a plan of campaign and to make Oxford a centre of the Apostolical propaganda. In the letter to Keble after the Hadleigh Conference from which I have already quoted, he writes : " I do not think we have yet made as much as we ought of our situation at Oxford, and of the deference paid to it through the country. Are not many eyes looking towards us everywhere, not as ' masters and scholars,' but as residents ; so that all our acts, as coming from the university, might have the authority of a vote of Convocation almost at such times when Convocation cannot be expected to speak out ? Now no party is likely to be active in Oxford but ourselves, so the field is before us. Do let us agree as to writing letters to our friends, just as if we were canvassing. Now if I could say that other persons agreed with me in thinking it desirable to say and do all in our power to stir up the Church, and if I knew the points of agreement—*i.e.*, if we were to settle on some uniform plan of talking as to principles, etc.—then I would not mind writing as in an election, canvassing, to men I know very little of. Pray think of this and send me a sketch of principles—*e.g.*, that by the Irish Bill the Church's liberties are invaded, etc. And should we not aim at getting up petitions next year to the King ? " [1]

This correspondence was followed by a meeting at Oxford between Newman, Froude, Keble, and Palmer, in order to draw up a basis of agreement such as Newman had suggested. Keble's suggestions, however, proved far too radical for Palmer and his friends, who were entirely opposed to any abandonment of the connexion with the State, and the draft that was finally approved in the autumn by Palmer and Newman as a basis for the proposed Association of Friends of the Church was an extremely moderate and non-committal document which contained no reference to Froude's distinctive principles. [2]

Meanwhile, however, Newman had set to work with Froude's help on the lines that he had described in his letter to Keble and had begun to canvas for the Apostolical cause throughout the country. [3] "The correspondence that ensued was immense," writes Thomas Mozley, who was one of Newman's most

[1] Newman, *Letters*, etc., I, p. 387.
[2] See the successive drafts, printed by Perceval in his collection of *Papers*, etc., pp. 11, 12 and 17.
[3] The way in which the campaign was organized is shown by the draft of Instructions to Propagandists printed in Newman's *Letters and Correspondence*, II. This quasi-political agitation contrasts so strongly with Newman's earlier and later views on ecclesiastical parties that one cannot fail to see in it a further proof of the influence of Froude's militant spirit.

active collaborators in the provinces, " Nobody was too humble in intellect or in clerical position not to be invited and enrolled as an ally. Men survive, or have but lately passed away, who can never have known what it was to share a glory and a greatness except at that happy time." [1]

The correspondence thus initiated became the starting point of the *Tracts for the Times*, which were originally brief and incisive statements of " apostolical " principles or appeals for immediate action, which were sent in parcels to the propagandists in the provinces to be distributed as widely as possible, like electioneering pamphlets. The first batch of Tracts which appeared at the beginning of September were all of them written by Newman himself, but, to a greater extent than any other of Newman's writings they bear the stamp of Hurrell Froude's spirit and opinions and prove how close was the collaboration at this vital moment between the two friends. Even in style, these early Tracts have more in common with the Spartan simplicity of Froude's bare logical statements than with Newman's literary form, and at times they seem to echo his very words and terms of expression. [2]

The first two Tracts contain the essential principle of the Oxford Movements : its appeal to apostolic authority and to the doctrine of the apostolical succes-

---

[1] T. Mozley, *Reminiscences*, I, p. 313.
[2] Compare, *e.g.*, the concluding paragraphs of either of the first two Tracts with those of Froude's article in the *British Magazine* for July, 1833. This resemblance is also shown by the fact that the authorship of Tract 8 has been attributed to both Newman and Froude indifferently. Tract 59, a characteristic example of Froude's style, is printed in the *Remains* as the concluding section of his " Remarks on State Interference in Matters Spiritual."

sion against the Erastianism of the supporters of the Establishment and the Liberalism of its opponents.

"Should the Government and Country so far forget their God as to cast off the Church, to deprive it of its temporal honours and substance, *on what* will you rest the claim of respect and attention which you make upon your flocks? Hitherto you have been upheld by your birth, your education, your wealth, your connexions; should these secular advantages cease, on what must Christ's ministers depend? Is not this a serious practical question? We know how miserable is the state of religious bodies not supported by the State. Look at the Dissenters on all sides of you, and you will see at once that their ministers, depending simply on the people became the *creatures* of the people. Are you content that this should be your case? Alas! can a greater evil befall Christians than for their teachers to be guided by them, instead of guiding? How can we ' hold fast the form of sound words ' and ' keep that which is committed to our trust,' if our influence is to depend simply on our popularity? Is it not our very office to *oppose* the world? How then can we allow ourselves to *court* it? to preach smooth things and prophesy deceits? to make the way of life easy to the rich and indolent, and to bribe the humbler classes by excitements and strong intoxicating doctrine? Surely it must not be so;—and the question recurs, on *what* are we to rest our authority when the State deserts us? "

The answer is clear—the apostolic rock on which our authority is built and the gift of the apostolic spirit conferred in ordination. All that was necessary was to bring this truth home to an age that had neglected and forgotten it. " Stir up the gift of God which is in you. Make much of it. Show your value of it. Keep it before your minds as an honourable badge, far higher than that secular respectability or cultivation, or polish or learning or rank which gives you a hearing with the many. Tell *them* of your gift. The times will soon drive you to do this, if you mean to be still anything. But wait not for the times. Do not be compelled, by the world's forsaking you, to recur as if unwillingly to the high source of your authority. Speak out now before you are forced, both as glorying in your privilege, and to ensure your rightful honour from your people. A notion has gone abroad, that they can take away your power. They think they have given and can take it away. They think that it lies in the Church property and they know that they have politically the power to confiscate that property. They have been deluded into a notion that present palpable usefulness, produceable results, acceptableness to your flocks, that these and such like are the tests of your Divine commission. Enlighten them in this matter. Exalt our Holy Fathers, the Bishops, as the Representatives of the Apostles and the Angels of the Churches ; and magnify your office as being ordained by them to take part in their Ministry." [1]

Nothing, it is clear, could be more loyal and deferential than the attitude of the writers of the Tracts towards the episcopate. But it may be doubted whether the rich and easy going " Angels of the Churches," who

[1] From Tract 1 : " Thoughts on the Ministerial Commission. Respectfully addressed to the Clergy."

feared for their plump revenues and their seats in the House of Lords, altogether appreciated so uncompromising a devotion. There was something more revolutionary in the doctrine of the *Tracts for the Times* than even the ecclesiastical programme of the Whigs.[1] No doubt they contained nothing that had not been said a hundred times before by High Churchmen. But while others may have said it, the Tractarians actually meant it. Men felt uneasily that the old weapons of forgotten controversies had suddenly become charged with live explosive. The " Z.'s " arose with one accord and began to bombard Palmer with expostulations and remonstrances. Palmer himself was enough of a Z. to take fright. He was alarmed at anything that would bring discredit on his beloved Association which Newman for his part regarded only as a potential vehicle for apostolic propaganda. Accordingly Palmer wrote to his friends washing his hands of the Tracts and disassociating himself from their authors. " Some anonymous Tracts," says he, " have been written by various persons and circulated among our friends as the works of individuals, and not authorized by the Association. They were not in fact

---

[1] T. Mozley writes, with his customary mixture of truth and exaggeration : " The Tracts preached what a King and a Primate had lost their heads for ; what the monarchy, the Church, the whole constitution and the greater part of the gentry had been overthrown for ; what afterwards Bishops and clergy had been cast out for, and the Convocation suspended a century for. These doctrines had been all but prohibited in the Church of England, as they probably would have remained to this day, had not the revolutionary aspect of the Reformed Parliament seemed to place the Church of England in the old dilemma between the bear closing up behind and the precipice yawning in front. The new teaching was accepted as a reactionary protest against the existing state of affairs and as affording the best basis for the impending general controversy."—*Reminiscences*, I, p. 408.

intended to be the Tracts of the Association, but they were not unnaturally confounded with it, and as they have been disapproved of by many we have discontinued circulating them. I beg to observe however that I am not aware of anything in their Tracts tending to separate Church and State, and so far from there being the least intention of the kind among our leading friends, I know that they are most strong supporters of the union. It is true that two or three excellent individuals may go rather far on this subject (I will in the strictest confidence mention Mr. ——, Mr. —— and Mr. ——. [? Froude, Keble and Perceval or Newman]), but at the same time you will recollect that it is impossible but that there must be varieties of opinion among the individuals of a large Association . . . and they are not, I may add, our most influential members. Circumstances, indeed, render it impossible that they should take a leading part." [1]

This shows how far removed were Palmer and his friends from the Oxford Movement itself. [2] But Newman was still anxious to collaborate with him and at one moment he seems actually to have consented to the suspension of the Tracts. [3] After Froude's return to Oxford in October, however, he took a much firmer line and wrote to Palmer on Oct. 24 criticizing the adoption of any form of fixed organization such as the Association. [4] But after Froude's final departure, he was again hard

[1] Palmer, *Narrative*, pp. 211–212 ; cf. pp. 210 and 225–228 for letters of protest.
[2] Palmer actually contributed one Tract (No. 15) to the series, in collaboration with Newman. This was the Tract to which Froude took such strong exception.
[3] Letter to Froude, Sept. 18 (*Letters*, I, p. 402).
[4] *Ibid.*, pp. 409–412.

pressed by Palmer and his party to abandon the Tracts, and writes to Froude in great perplexity : " I am in the midst of troubles and no one but such οὐτιδανοὶ as Rogers to consult with. Palmer musters the Z's in great force against the Tracts and some Evangelicals. He presses and I am quite ready to admit a disclaimer (in the shape of a circular) of the Tracts. But he goes further, and wishes us to stop them. . . . What will be done I know not ; but I want advice sadly. I have no confidence in anyone. If I could be sure of five or six vigorous co-operators in various parts, I would laugh at opposition ; but I fear being beaten from the field. Keble says we *must* be read, unless we grow stupid, but I am not sure of our fertility even.

" The tracts are certainly liked in many places : among other persons by the Bishop of Winchester (Sumner). O that he would take us up ! I would go the length of my tether to meet him. . . . Evangelicals, as I anticipated, are struck with ' The Law of Liberty ' (Tract 8) and ' The Sin of the Church ' (Tract 6). The subject of Discipline too (I cannot doubt) will take with them. Surely my game lies with them. I can make no hand of the Z's. . . . I do think our Tracts, if we persist, will catch all the enthusiastic people among the Associated ; which will be wretched for the Z's. . . .

" My dear Froude,—I do so fear I may be self willed in this matter of the Tracts. Pray do advise me according to your light." [1]

Froude's advice was definite enough. " I would not

[1] *Ibid.*, pp. 420–423 (Nov. 13).

have had a hand in printing that Address " (Palmer's Address to the Archbishop). " As to giving up the Tracts, the notion is odious." " We must throw the Z's overboard." " Don't spend any of your money on such stuff as this Address again ; say, ' settle it among yourselves, gentlemen.' " [1]

From this point Newman seems to have felt no more hesitations and to have made up his mind to follow an independent line. A week later we find him writing to his friend Rickards : " As to our present doings, we are set off, and with God's speed we shall go forward through evil report and good report, through real and supposed blunders. We are as men climbing a rock, who tear clothes and flesh, and slip now and again, and yet make progress, and are careless that bystanders criticize, so that their cause gains while they lose. We are set out, and we have funds for the present ; which like the widows' cruise shall not fail. This then is our position, connected with no association, answerable to no one except God and His Church, committing no one, bearing the blame, doing the work. I trust I speak sincerely in saying I am willing that it be said I go too far, so that I push on the cause of truth some little way. Surely it is energy that gives edge to any undertaking and energy is ever incautious and exaggerated. . . . Be it so ; it is well to fall, if you kill your adversary. Nor can I wish anyone a happier lot than to be himself unfortunate, yet to urge on a triumphant cause ; like Laud and Ken in their day, who left a name which after-ages censure or pity, but whose works do follow them. Let it be

[1] *Ibid.*, p. 426, and Froude's *Remains*, I, pp. 331–333 (Nov. 17).

the lot of those I love to live in the heart of one or two in each succeeding generation, or to be altogether forgotten, while they have helped forward the truth." [1]

The letter was written the day before Froude left England for Barbados, and as Newman wrote the last lines he must have been thinking of his friend, who was forced to leave the ranks at the moment when the fight was hottest.

And yet, though Newman now realized that there could be little hope of his friend's ultimate recovery, he refused to admit that Froude's genius could be wasted. His undying spirit of love and confidence finds utterance in one of the rare passionate outbursts of his letters to Froude written nearly a year later. " It is quite impossible that some way or other you are not destined to be the instrument of God's purposes. Though I saw the earth cleave, and you fall in, or Heaven open, and a chariot appear, I should say just the same. God has ten thousand posts of service. You might be of use in the central elemental fire ; you might be of use in the depths of the sea." [2]

And in a sermon at St. Mary's, written at the end of the year, he speaks in the same way regarding the loss of " friends or of especially gifted men who seem in their day the earthly support of the Church." " They are taken away for some purpose surely ; their gifts are not lost to us ; their soaring minds, the fire of their contemplations, the sanctity of their desires, the vigour of their faith, the sweetness and gentleness of their affections were not given without an object." They

---

[1] *Ibid.*, pp. 429-430 (Nov. 22).
[2] *Letters* II, p. 67.

are like Moses on the mountain, whose prayers turn the tide of battle in the plain below.[1]

Certainly with Froude's departure, it was as though his spirit entered into Newman, giving him a self reliance and a power of leadership such as he had never known hitherto. Newman himself was conscious of this, and one cannot but think that he had it in his mind when, about this time, he described the relation between St. Gregory Nazianzen and his friend St. Basil, in *The Church of the Fathers*: " Gregory," he writes, " disliked the routine intercourse of society, he disliked ecclesiastical business, he disliked publicity, he disliked strife . . . he loved the independence of solitude, the tranquillity of private life, leisure for meditation, reflection, self government, study and literature. He admired yet he playfully satirized Basil's lofty thoughts and herioc efforts. Yet upon Basil's death, Basil's spirit, as it were, came into him. . . . Was it Gregory or was it Basil that blew the trumpet in Constantinople, and waged a successful war in the very seat of the enemy, in spite of all his fluctuations of mind, misgivings, fastidiousness, disgust with self, and love of quiet ? Such was the power of the great Basil, triumphing in his death though failing throughout his life. Within four or five years of his departure to his reward, all the objects were either realized, or in the way to be realized, which he had vainly attempted, or sadly waited for. His eyes had failed in longing, they waited for the Morning, and death closed them ere it came." [2]

[1] *Parochial Sermons*, II, xviii (Mysteries in Religion).
[2] *Historical Studies*, II, p. 76. The parallel has been pointed out by the late Louise Imogen Guiney in her book on Hurrell Froude, p. 166 (1904).

VII. *FROM THE* VIA MEDIA *TO* THE IDEAL OF A CHRISTIAN CHURCH

SEPARATION

Do not their souls, who 'neath the Altar wait
  Until their second birth,
The gift of patience need, as separate
  From their first friends of earth ?
Not that earth's blessings are not all outshone
  By Eden's Angel flame,
But that earth knows not yet, the Dead has won
  That crown, which was his aim.
For when he left it, 'twas a twilight scene
  About his silent bier,
A breathless struggle, faith and sight between,
  And Hope and sacred Fear.
Fear startled at his pains and dreary end,
  Hope raised her chalice high,
And the twin-sisters still his shade attend,
  Viewed in the mourner's eye.

So day by day for him from earth ascends,
  As dew in summer-even,
The speechless intercession of his friends,
  Toward the azure heaven.
Ah ! dearest, with a word he could dispel
  All questioning, and raise
Our hearts to rapture, whispering all was well,
  And turning prayer to praise.
And other secrets too he could declare,
  By patterns all divine,
His earthly creed retouching here and there,
  And deepening every line.
Dearest ! he longs to speak, as I to know,
  And yet we both refrain :
It were not good ; a little doubt below,
  And all will soon be plain.

J. H. N.,
MARSEILLES, *June* 27, 1833.

(This was the last of the poems composed by Newman during his Mediterranean journey. But the twelve concluding lines were added in 1836 on Froude's death.)

THE three years 1834—1836 saw the steady ripening of Newman's genius and the triumphant progress of the Oxford Movement from small beginnings till it became a power in the Church of England. It was the beginning of the seven years to which Newman always looked back as the happiest time of his life, a time of sunshine and plenty, during which, as he says in the *Apologia*, he tried to lay up as much as he could for the lean years that were to follow. During these years he laid the foundations of a new theology for the Church of England, which has had an incalculable influence on the development of modern Anglicanism, and which perhaps still remains the best justification for the essential Anglican position. Newman differed from the other leaders of the revival, except Froude, in his sense of the need for a consistent and systematic intellectual basis for his beliefs. He was not content with the pure traditionalism of the Kebles and Isaac Williams or with the more emotional fideism of Pusey. He had acquired from his studies in the Church of the Fathers the old Catholic conception of theological dogma as a definite organized body of religious truth, and to neglect this body of truth seemed to him not merely a sin against faith but an offence against reason.

" Diminution from the stock of knowledge is commonly considered a loss in this day ; yet, strange to say, in the instance before us, it is thought far otherwise. The great mass of educated men are at once uneasy, impatient, and irritated, not simply incredulous, directly they are promised, from any quarter, some clear view of the original and apostolic doctrine, to them unknown, on any subject of religion. . . . They sanction a rule of philosophy which they

practically refute every time they praise Newton or
Cuvier. In truth, they can endure a positive theory of
knowledge in other provinces of knowledge ; but in
theology they prefer knowledge to be vague, specula-
tive and indeterminate." [1] Newman believed that the
preservation of this corpus of theological truth was the
essential note of the true Church and that it was to be
found most perfectly in the Anglican Church. Rome
had added to it, Protestantism had subtracted from it,
only in the Church of England was there to be found
the safe middle way of Catholic orthodoxy—the
Apostolic Church and the Faith of the Fathers.
Actually, of course, he admitted that the Church of
England had gravely compromised her position by
the practical toleration of Protestant error and by the
neglect of her Catholic heritage. Nevertheless she
could not forfeit it entirely without losing her own
identity. The Anglican position was essentially bound
up with the maintenance of this objective body of
truth which was neither Protestant nor Roman but
purely Catholic, and all that was necessary was for
her to return to her original basis and to vindicate her
rightful inheritance.

This is Newman's theory of the *Via Media*, which,
in spite of superficial resemblances, is entirely different
from the other Tractarian theory of the Church—
the Branch Theory—which was put forward by William
Palmer at about the same date,[2] and which is often
regarded as the official doctrine of the High Church

---

[1] *Lectures on the Prophetical Office of the Church*, 2nd ed. (1838), pp. 4–5.
[2] Palmer's *Treatise on the Church of Christ*, 1838. Professor Brilioth
describes this work, not altogether without reason, as " one of the most
narrow-minded productions of Anglican theology."

party. This theory regards Catholic dogma not as a fixed norm of orthodoxy, but as the common denominator or highest common factor of the various branches of the Church that retain episcopal orders. The practical advantage of this theory is that it avoids any strict definition of the dogmatic standard of orthodoxy, since the latter expands automatically with the growing divergences of the different forms of Christianity, but this, as Newman pointed out, is also its fatal weakness since it makes truth dependent on ecclesiastical frontiers and asserts that the one true Church has one teaching in England and another in Italy. It stands or falls with the paradox that two societies which excommunicate one another and regard each other as mutually exclusive are, nevertheless, one society and form part of one visible and indivisible Church.

Moreover, the Branch Theory also suffers from the fact that it affords no true *locus standi* against Rome. In the eyes of a man like Palmer, to leave the Church of England for the Church of Rome was a damnable act of apostasy, but considered in the light of his own theory it would seem to be a very small matter indeed—nothing more, in fact, than a mere change of perch, from one branch to another. And as the true faith is the faith that is common to the Churches, there can be no sin against faith in a change of allegiance : it is, at most, a breach of discipline. The *Via Media*, on the other hand, does give the Church of England a certain theological status and makes it

---

[1] " Palmer's View of Faith and Unity " in *Essays, Critical and Historical*, I, v.

possible to meet Rome and Geneva on their own ground—the ground of religious truth. Unlike the modern Anglo-Catholic, Newman, at least in his earlier writings, does not attempt to explain away the Reformation, and he realizes that a change of fundamental and so revolutionary a character can only be justified on the plea of dire necessity, since it involved the sacrifice of so much that is admirable in the Catholic tradition. " When we left her, she suffered us not to go in the beauty of holiness, we left our garments and fled." [1] " And truly when one surveys the grandeur of their system a sigh arises in the thoughtful mind, to think that we should be separate from them : Cam talis esses, utinam noster esses !—But alas AN UNION IS IMPOSSIBLE. Their communion is infected with heterodoxy ; we arc bound to flee it as a pestilence. They have established a lie in the place of God's truth, and by their claim of immutability in doctrine, cannot undo the sin they have committed. They cannot repent. Popery must be destroyed ; it cannot be reformed." [2]

Strong as this language is, it is entirely in harmony with Anglican tradition and, as Newman remarked, it has the consensus of Anglican divines behind it. The weakness of the *Via Media* lies rather on the opposite side—in the lack of a definite frontier against Protestantism and in its historical failure to realize itself in practice. It may be plausibly maintained that it is only a paper theory, which is to be found more in books than in the existing system of the Established Church.

[1] " Home Thoughts from Abroad " in *the British Magazine*, Vol. V, p. 130 (February, 1834).
[2] Tract 20. " The Visible Church," Pt. III (Dec. 24, 1833).

" Protestantism and Popery are real religions ; no one can doubt about them ; they have furnished the mould in which nations have been cast ; but the *Via Media*, viewed as an integral system, has scarcely had existence except on paper, it has never been reduced to practice, but by piecemeal ; it is known not positively, but negatively, in its differences from the rival creeds not in its own properties, and can only be described as a third system, neither the one nor the other, partly both, cutting between them, and, as if with a critical fastidiousness, trifling with them both, and boasting to be nearer Antiquity than either." [1]

Newman admits to a great extent the force of this objection. " It still remains to be tried," he writes, " whether what is called Anglo-Catholicism, the religion of Andrewes, Laud, Hammond, Butler and Wilson, is capable of being professed, acted on and maintained on a large sphere of action and through a sufficient period, or whether it be a mere modification or transition state either of Romanism or of popular Protestantism according as we view it." [2]

Consequently Newman's adhesion to the theory of the *Via Media* always had a somewhat tentative and provisional character. His fundamental act of faith was in the Apostolic Church and the Church of the Fathers, and he believed in the Church of England only in so far and so long as it confined its teaching to that of Antiquity. In this he differed from Keble and Pusey, whose faith in the Church of England was primary and absolute. Pusey has related how in the

---

[1] *The Prophetical Office of the Church*, 2nd ed., p. 20.
[2] *Op. cit.*, pp. 21–22.

days of the crisis Newman said to him, " O Pusey, we have leant on the Bishops and they have broken under us," and he adds, " I never leant on the Bishops, I leant on the Church of England." But for Newman this attitude was impossible, because to him the validity of his theory depended on its being recognized as the official doctrine of the Church of England, and if it was once disavowed by the Bishops it became no more than a private opinion—a " paper theory."

To us who judge after the event, the failure of Newman's hopes may seem a foregone conclusion, but at the time this was by no means obvious. The Anglican reaction against the movement of Liberal reform was for the moment so strong as to deceive even independent observers. A rising politician like Disraeli could speak of the Church as " the most powerful agent in the previous development of England and the most efficient means of the renovation of the national spirit," and could join with the Tractarians in asserting " the paramount character of the ecclesiastical policy and the majesty of the Theocratic Principle." [1]

If the Church was to be once more an independent force in national life, it was absolutely necessary for it to possess a definite programme and a distinctive intellectual position, and where could this be found save in the doctrine of the *Via Media*, which claimed, with some justice, to represent the classical tradition of 17th century Anglicanism, while at the same time it

[1] Preface to *Coningsby*. Disraeli was evidently a student of Froude's *Remains*. Not only is Coningsby's diatribe against Conservatism and Erastianism in Book VII, Chapter ii, thoroughly Froudian in spirit, but he uses the arguments and even the actual words of Froude's " Remarks on State Interference in Matters Spiritual." Cp. Froude's *Remains*, III, pp. 198–207, and *Coningsby*, p. 350 (World's Classics ed. (1931)).

was capable, as the Tractarians showed, of being adapted to the needs of the existing situation ? What the Tractarians did not realize was that it was the very lack of definite principles that was the salvation of the Church of England. When she professed the doctrines of the *Via Media* she passed through two successive revolutions and had only escaped complete shipwreck by abandoning the principles of Laud and Sancroft and acquiescing in the inglorious compromise of the Revolution settlement. It was not to be wondered at that the Anglican episcopate should refuse to risk a fresh conflict with the victorious forces of parliamentary Liberalism in an age when she no longer had the monarchy behind her and could only rely on the support of a handful of disinterested idealists. Newman, however, cared little for the practical responsibilities of the ecclesiastical politician. He could understand intellectual moderation and finesse, but not the sacrifice of intellectual principles to social expediency. For him the real dilemma was an interior one between his vision of the Catholic Church as a historical reality, an objective power that demanded an unconditional allegiance and the Protestant influences that still coloured his outlook, above all with regard to the Roman Church and the Papacy. Ever since his Mediterranean journey his mind had been fascinated and tormented by the spectacle of Rome.

> How shall I name Thee, Light of the wide West
> Or heinous error-seat ?

he asks in the verses that he wrote at Rome in 1834.

Was this the living Church in all the majesty of its imperial claims and the mystery of its sacramental power, or was it rather an Antichristian power, the mystery of Iniquity, an evil principle seated in the very heart of the Church? Each of these alternatives had the weight of a great historic tradition behind it, for the identification of Rome with Antichrist had been the common teaching of all the Protestant Churches since the time of Luther and Calvin. It was the paradox of Newman's thought, however, that he accepted both these alternatives simultaneously.

Rome remained a part of the true Church, and yet at the same time she was the servant of Antichrist. "For, in truth, she is a Church beside herself," he writes in a curious passage of his *Lectures on the Prophetical Office of the Church*,[1] "abounding in noble gifts and rightful titles, but unable to use them religiously; crafty, obstinate, wilful, malicious, cruel, unnatural as madmen are, or rather she may be said to resemble a demoniac, possessed with principles, powers and tendencies not his own; in outward form and in natural powers what God has made her, but ruled within by an inexorable spirit, who is sovereign in his management of her and most subtle and most successful in the use of her gifts."

This strange imagination, dark with the accumulated hatred and suspicion of centuries of religious warfare, had an extraordinary hold on Newman, and it was the last and not the least of Hurrell Froude's services to

---

[1] *Prophetical Office of the Church*, p. 103. There is a remarkable similarity between Newman's views in this passage and the original Calvinist doctrine. According to Calvin, the Catholic Church is still the Church, though it is in captivity to Antichrist, in the same way that Israel remained the people of God, even when it had fallen into idolatry under the rule of wicked kings.

the Oxford Movement that he helped to free the mind of his friend from this obsession. Of all the Tractarians, Froude has the most right to the title of Anglo-Catholic. For while both Keble and Newman were preoccupied with the apologetic task of proving the Anglican Church to be truly Catholic, Froude was only concerned to follow Catholic principles to their legitimate conclusion whatever the effect might be on the Anglican position. During the last years of his life, and especially during the time of his exile in the West Indies, he emancipated himself more and more from Keble's influence and developed his own principles independently. His attitude to the Roman Church gradually became more benevolent, while his criticisms of the Protestantism and Erastianism of the Established Church grew steadily stronger.[1] In his first letter from Barbados on Jan. 9, 1834, he writes to Keble : " You will be shocked by my avowal that I am every day becoming a less and less loyal son of the Reformation. It appears to me plain that in all matters that seem to us indifferent or even doubtful, we should conform our practices to those of the Church that has preserved its traditionary practices unbroken. We cannot know about any seemingly indifferent practice

[1] One of the writers in a recent volume of studies in the Oxford Movement (*Northern Catholicism*, p. 21) quotes the following sentence from one of Froude's letters from Barbados as proving Froude's anti-Roman sentiments : " The more I read the more I am reconciled to the present state of things in England and the prospects of the Church." Unfortunately he does not complete his quotation which is a typical example of Froude's ironic manner. " *It seems to be only the fermentation of filth which has long been in existence and could not be got rid of otherwise.*" I am afraid that Froude would regard this method of quotation as another instance of the " δικονουία and φενακισμὸς " which he so deplored in the anti-Roman *Tracts for the Times !*

of the Church of Rome that it is not a development of
the Apostolic ἦθος ; and it is to no purpose to say that
we can find no proof of it in the writings of the six first
centuries ; they must find a *dis*proof if they would do
anything." [1]

And again, a year later : " And first I shall attack
you for the expression ' The Church teaches ' so and so,
which I observe is in the Tract equivalent to ' The
Prayer Book, etc., teaches us ' so and so. . . . Why is
the opinion of the English clergy, since the enactment
of the Prayer-Book, entitled to be called the teaching
of the Church more than that of the clergy of the sixteen
previous centuries ; or again than the clergy of France,
Italy, Spain, Russia, etc., etc. ? I can see no other
claim which the Prayer-Book has on a layman's
deference, as the teaching of the Church, which the
Breviary and Missal have not in a far greater degree." [2]

In the same way he writes to Newman, protesting
against the " Tract Protestantism," the reprinting of
" Poor Bishop Cosin " against Trans-substantiation, and
what he considers the unfairness and sophistry of the
defence of Anglican claims in Tract 15. He even
begins to have some misgivings on the perfection of his
former heroes, Laud and the Nonjurors : " Must it
not be owned that the Church of England saints are,
with a few rare exceptions, deficient in the austere
beauty of the Catholic ἦθος ? Keble will be severe on
me for this, but I cannot deny that Laud's archi-
tecture seems to me typical." [3]

---

[1] *Remains*, I, p. 336.
[2] *Ibid.*, pp. 401–403 (Feb. 25, 1835).
[3] *Ibid.*, p. 422 (Nov. 1, 1835).

But, above all, he attacks Newman for his attitude to the Roman Church. He had already criticized the first part of " Home Thoughts from Abroad " for its Protestant " slang " and " name-calling," and in 1835 he writes even more strongly against Newman's attitude to Rome in the *Via Media* Tracts : " I must enter another protest against your cursing and swearing as you do. What good can it do ?—and I call it uncharitable to an excess. How mistaken we may ourselves be on many points that are only gradually opening on us ! Surely you should reserve ' blasphemous,' ' impious,' etc., for denial of the articles of the Faith." [1]

When Froude wrote these words he was back again in England, arriving at Oxford in time to take part in the voting on the proposal to abolish the religious test at matriculation. Years afterwards Anne Mozley described how she saw him there for the first and last time : " terribly thin, his countenance dark and wasted, but with a brilliancy of expression and a grace of outline which justified all that his friends had said of him. He was in the theatre next day, entering into all the enthusiasm of the scene, and shouting ' *Non placet* ' with all his friends about him. While he lived at all he must live his life." [2]

Never, in fact, was Froude more himself, more active in mind and more capable of influencing others

---

[1] *Ibid.*, p. 395 (Jan. 1835). Cf. *The Letters of Lord Blachford* (F. B. Rogers), pp. 45–46. " (Froude) said to me of Laud that all he saw in him was that he was a *brave* man with some good views, adding that all our divines since the Reformation had been very dark about Church Independence." (Letter to Newman, Nov. 27, 1837.)

[2] A. Mozley in *Letters and Correspondence of J. H. Newman*, II, p. 95.

than in those last months : " . . . his unconquerable energy of mind triumphed over weakness and decay, till men with all their health and strength about them might gaze upon his attenuated form, struck with a certain awe of wonderment at the brightness of his wit, the intenseness of his mental vision and the iron strength of his argument." [1]

Newman paid his last visit to Dartington in September. " I left and took my last farewell of R.H.F. on Sunday, Oct. 11, in the evening. When I took leave of him, his face lighted up and almost shone in the darkness, as if to say that in this world we were parting for ever." [2]

It is not to be wondered at that the last letters and words of such a friend should have had a powerful influence on Newman's mind. " When a man in whom dwells God's grace is lying on the bed of suffering," he says in one of his sermons, " or when he has been stripped of his friends and is solitary, he has, in a special way, tasted of the powers of the world to come, and exhorts and consoles with authority." [3] And in the years that followed Froude's death, as Newman meditated over the letters and sayings of his friend, which he and Keble were preparing to publish, this influence grew rather than diminished. In their minds, Froude became canonized as the saint of the movement and the perfect example of Tractarian ethos, and his lightest word carried weight. This could not but tend gradually to weaken Newman's confidence in the

[1] T. Mozley in *British Critic*, April, 1840.
[2] *Letters*, II, p. 122.
[3] *Parochial Sermons*, V, xxi. " Affliction a School of Comfort " (Oct. 19, 1834)

validity of the *Via Media*. For while it was the essence of that theory to keep an even course between the Scylla of Protestantism and the Roman Charybdis, Froude's influence steadily deflected it away from Protestantism towards an integral Catholicism. Froude had never had any sympathy with a policy of moderation and compromise. His way was not a *Via Media*, but a *Via Ultima*, a steep and narrow way which went straight ahead to its goal without turning aside for any obstacle. And this Froudian extremism was really more characteristic of the original spirit of the Oxford Movement, as shown in *Lyra Apostolica* and the first *Tracts for the Times*, than the *Via Media* itself.

But while this appealed to one side of Newman's mind it did not gain his full assent. Newman was a cautious thinker, who refused to take his fences after Froude's headlong fashion or to go forward until he had surveyed his ground carefully. Nothing could be more mistaken than the view so frequently heard of late that Newman's conversion did not rest on theological reasons, but was due to a sudden emotional crisis.[1] His abandonment of the *Via Media*, far from being a sudden flight, was a slow and hard-fought retreat in which he stubbornly contested every inch of the ground. As early as 1835 the battle was opened in his correspondence with the Abbé Jager, and already at that time in his argument with Froude on Tradition, and in the second part of his *Home Thoughts from Abroad*, we see the emergence of

[1] *E.g.*, F. L. Cross, *John Henry Newman*, pp. 130–144. G. Faber, *Oxford Apostles*, pp. 413–416, 448–449. Whatever we may think of Newman's thesis, there is no denying the cogency and the consistency of his argument in the *Essay on Development*, and I do not think that anyone who has read the book will agree with Mr. Faber's summary dismissal of it as a " piece of magnificent rhetoric."

the central issue—the conflict between the static and the dynamic conceptions of Catholicism—which was to occupy his mind until he found his definitive solution ten years later in *The Essay on the Development of Christian Doctrine*. If Froude had lived it is possible that the conflict would have been shorter, for his sympathies were distinctly with the dynamic conception of the Church,[1] and his refusal to anathematize Roman doctrines and his tendency to look on existing Catholic practice as the expression of the mind of the living Church, could not fail to tell against the *Via Media*.

On the other hand, at the very time when Froude was removed, the cause of the *Via Media* found a powerful ally in Dr. Pusey, who from about the year 1835 becomes one of the central figures in the Oxford Movement. He had long been a friend of Newman's, but he stood apart from the original Tractarian group. He was generally regarded as a moderate Liberal who sympathized with the tendencies of modern German theology, and when H. J. Rose published his attack on the rationalism of the German theologians, Pusey came to the rescue in an essay which he feared would earn him the reputation of being " one-third mystic, one-third rationalist and one-third a Methodist, though I am none of the three." [2] How far his religious views at this time were from those which he afterwards came to represent may be seen in his letters to his fiancée. For example, in reply to a question about St. Catherine of Siena, he writes : " Your namesake, about whose vision you enquire, was probably a half

---

[1] Cf. his letter to Keble, *supra*, p. 110.
[2] *Life of Pusey*, I, by Liddon, etc., p. 153.

distracted visionary and vision-seeing mystic. How far knavery may have mingled with her fanaticism, or whether she was only employed as an instrument by others, can probably not be decided." [1] Gradually, however, he became more and more favourable to the views of Newman and Keble, [2] and by the time of the publication of the first Tracts he ranked as an independent sympathizer. His first Tract (No. 18 on Fasting) was signed with his initials in order to safeguard his independence, and it was not until the publication of his important Tract on Baptism, in 1835, that he became thoroughly identified with the movement. His university status as a professor and his social position as the younger son of a well-known county family gave him the external prestige which Newman and Froude had lacked, and from the year 1836 he took the place of Hurrell Froude as the chief coadjutor of Newman and Keble in the direction of the movement.

Pusey was in almost all things the extreme opposite to Froude. All his characteristic qualities—his learning, his orthodoxy, his gravity, his solidity—were *heavy* qualities. Even Isaac Williams, who was by no means frivolous, found himself " silenced by so awful a person," while his " presence always checked Newman's lighter and unrestrained mood." [3] While Froude expressed his deepest convictions in epigrammatic slang, Pusey's letters were apt to become theological treatises. One thing only they had in common :

---

[1] *Ibid.*, p. 131.

[2] At the close of 1832 he can still speak of Calvin as a saint, though in deference to Newman's views he substituted " giant " for " saint " when he published the letter in question.

[3] *The Autobiography of Isaac Williams*, p. 70.

both were ascetics ; in fact they were the two pioneers of Anglican asceticism. Even here, however, there was a characteristic difference between the two. While Froude carried off his ascetism with an air of gay indifference, Pusey persecuted his nature with the sombre determination of a Jansenist. Yet one cannot but feel that the smiling irony of Froude's humorous self-contempt pierced deeper than the type of asceticism which shows itself in Pusey's resolution never to lie down in his bed without remembering that he was unworthy to lie down except in hell, never to smile unless duty commanded it, and " to drink cold water at dinner, as only fit to be where there is not a drop to cool this flame." [1]

This extreme asceticism, however, belongs to the later phase of Pusey's career, after his wife's death and the loss of Newman, when his cell at Christ Church (for he lived in almost monastic seclusion) was the rallying point of the remaining forces of the Oxford Movement. In the earlier years, down to 1839, he still took an active part in social life, and his moral weight and his reputation for learning tended to give the movement a more moderate and established character than it had previously possessed. It was he who changed the character of the *Tracts for the Times*, transforming them from brief and provocative statements of principle into long and, it must be admitted, dull theological treatises. He brought up the heavy batteries of patristic learning and inaugurated the great series of translations of patristic works—the Library of the Fathers—which was to continue for nearly fifty years,

[1] *Life of Pusey*, III, 105-8.

Pusey was, in short, the perfect embodiment of the *Via Media*, and it seemed as though his influence would give the movement an established and almost official character. A visitor to Oxford in 1837 writes that " it is allowed that the Doctor (Pusey) and Newman *governed the University*, and that nothing could withstand the influence of themselves and their friends."

Never was the literary activity of the movement greater. It now possessed its official review in the *British Critic*, which was edited by Newman, and afterwards by T. Mozley. Theological and controversial works poured from the press, and the Tracts sold 60,000 a year. At this moment, however, the irrepressible Froude intervened once more and ruined the reputation of the movement for respectability and moderation by a reassertion of all the revolutionary elements that were implicit in the Tractarian position. From the standpoint of the *Via Media*, the publication of Froude's *Remains* was the greatest tactical mistake in the history of the movement. It alienated the sympathy of moderate High Churchmen and aroused the suspicion and hostility of its opponents. A representative of the former class, Samuel Wilberforce, writes in his diary : " Read a little of Froude's ' Journals.' They are most instructive to me ; will exceedingly discredit Church principles and show an amazing want of Christianity, so far." [1] While an Oxford Evangelical, the Rev. Peter Maurice, remarked that " they cannot but fill the heart of every true Christian with horror and his eyes with tears." " They afford evidences of what the human mind (even with

[1] *Life of Samuel Wilberforce*, I.

all the advantages of natural talent and education) may be brought to, when not guided by the Light which is from above." [1]

And yet the intentions of the editors, Keble and Newman, were so pathetically well meaning. They hoped that Froude's letters with their hatred of pretence and humbug would prove an antidote to the formalism and priggishness that had begun to creep into the movement as it became fashionable and would give the new generation of Anglo-Catholics a vivid idea of the true Tractarian ethos. They thought that the intimacy of Hurrell's self-revelation would disarm criticism and that everyone would be attracted by his originality and charm. Newman writes to Keble : " I have transcribed the ' Private Thoughts,' and am deeply impressed with their attractive character. They are full of instruction and interest, as I think all will feel. . . . We see his mind only breaking out into more original and beautiful discoveries, from that very repression which at first sight seemed likely to be the utter prohibition to exercise his special powers. He used playfully to say that ' his highest ambition was to be a humdrum,' and by relinquishing the prospect of originality he has but become more original." [2]

Actually, however, this affectionate tribute to the memory of a dead friend exploded like a bomb and aroused more alarm in the hostile camp than all the volumes of controversial divinity that the movement had produced. Speeches were made upon it in the

[1] Quoted by L. I. Guiney in " Hurrell Froude," p. 407, from *A Key to the Popery of Oxford*, by Peter Maurice.
[2] *Letters*, II, p. 211 (June 30, 1837).

House of Commons, Bishops censured it in their charges and professors of divinity in their sermons. Froude's most private thoughts and most intimate confessions were exposed to the derision of fools and the scandal of pious respectability.

Yet one cannot think that Froude himself would have regretted it. His ironic self-depreciation could have found no better monument than this posthumous exposure which discomfited his opponents at the same time that it humiliated himself. It saved the movement from becoming prematurely respectable, while at the same time giving it a fresh impulse towards the Catholic ideal. For Newman's hopes were not entirely deceived. The publication of the *Remains* did attract enthusiasts, and did more than anything else to create that new school of thorough-going Anglo-Catholics which had so great an influence on the later history of the Movement.[1] The articles in the *British Critic* of 1840–41, which were the first manifestos of this school— notably Oakeley's essay on Jewel, and Ward's essay on Arnold—show the influence of the *Remains* on almost every page. Oakeley had been a friend of Froude's before he was himself associated with the Movement, and in later days he used to recall Froude's words to him : " My dear O. I believe you will come right some day, but you are a long time about it." Ward, on the other hand, had no personal knowledge of Froude, but he owed his conversion to the Movement to Froude's writings. " Out came *Froude*," writes Ward to Pusey, " of which it is little to say that it delighted me more than any book of the kind I ever read,"

[1] See note at end of chapter.

" This is what I have been looking for," he said. " Here is a man who knows what he means and says it. This is the man for me ! He speaks out." [1]

The conversion of Ward was no small achievement, for he was one of the most brilliant of the younger dons, and came straight from the opposite camp. He occupies somewhat the same position in the later history of the movement that Froude occupied in its earlier stages. It is true that he had not the same ethos— there was nothing of what Isaac Williams calls " the Fairfield and Bisley spirit " about him. His masters were Bentham and John Stuart Mill rather than Keble. But he had the same love of talk and epigram, the same keen wit, the same remorseless logic and the same hatred of humbug and pomposity ; only he carried Froude's originality to eccentricity, and Froude's humour to buffoonery. Froude had criticized the *Via Media*, but Ward kicked it to pieces and executed a dialectical *pas seul* among the ruins. Nevertheless it can hardly be denied that *The Ideal of a Christian Church*—that vast and amorphous pamphlet which was the ultimate *pierre d'achoppement* of the Oxford Movement—was a legitimate child of the Oxford Movement and the logical culmination of Froude's own thought. Froude's reaction against Conservatism and Erastianism—his ideal of the Church as a society at once theocratic and democratic—was based not on sociological considerations, as with Lamennais and de Maistre, but on his intense thirst for personal holiness ; the supernatural authority of the Church was, in his eyes, the necessary corollary of the supernatural life of

[1] W. Ward, *William George Ward and the Oxford Movement*, p. 84.

the Christian. And this conception, which is also implicit in Newman's sermons, was worked out systematically and completely in Ward's book. His theory of the Church is not a juridical one like Palmer's, or a theological one, like the *Via Media*, but a moral one, which finds its supreme criterion in conscience and religious experience. " No mathematical axiom," he writes, " is more certain than this moral one that where the fruits of holiness show themselves, there is the Holy Ghost, and there is really [so far as it goes] *true doctrine*." [1] For where the spiritual life is strong, there the life of faith is strong, and where the latter is corrupted the former withers away. Moreover, the true Church is not only the mother of the saints, she is also the mother of the poor, and it is the neglect of the sufferings of the poor which roused Ward's indignation most against contemporary English religion.

Thus his indictment of the Church of England is primarily a moral one, and he sums it up under the following heads : 1. Absence of all system of moral discipline for the poor. 2. Absence of all system of moral discipline for the rich. 3. Our Church's total neglect of her duties as guardian and witness to morality. 4. Our Church's total neglect of her duties as witness and teacher of orthodoxy. 5. Powerlessness of our Church to perform her other duties, especially in helping and protecting the poor, while those are neglected. 6. Rationalism prevalent in our Church." [2]

This was turning the tables with a vengeance on the

[1] *The Ideal of a Christian Church*, p. 207, quoted from Ward's article in the *British Critic*, 1841, p. 335.
[2] *The Ideal of a Christian Church*, Chapter VI.

self-righteous insularity of Victorian Protestantism, more especially since Ward went on to find his " ideal " exemplified not in the Church of the Fathers, as with Newman, nor in the mediæval Church, as with Froude, but in modern Catholicism and in the lives and teachings of the counter-reformation saints. Nevertheless, it is the logical culmination of one element in the movement, an element that had first showed itself in Froude's drastic anti-Protestantism and in his exaltation of the ascetic ideals of Catholic sanctity. As the modern Swedish historian of the Oxford Movement, Dr. Brilioth, has written : " It is a fact of the greatest moment for the historical comprehension of the Neo-Anglican Movement, that the one-sided (*sic*) emphasis laid on holiness with its corollaries in the requirement of authority, obedience and asceticism, and along with them a certain measure of æstheticism (not only aiming at ' the beauty of holiness,') that these in a logical exposition, such as Ward's book aims at being, seems to point so directly to the Roman system. This answers in a manner that is more than accidental to the Romanising tendency which ever more strongly appeared in the later history of Neo-Anglicanism." [1]

The same tendency shows itself in Newman during these years, though Newman was following a somewhat different path to the same goal. The *Via Media* had disappeared and left him in the wilderness, repudiated by the University which he had hoped to make the instrument of the regeneration of the Church of England, and by the Bishops whose apostolic authority he had championed. In this crisis, when the external

[1] Y. Brilioth, *The Anglican Revival*, p. 272.

notes of the Church seemed to have failed and when
the old landmarks of the *Via Media* had disappeared,
it was to the internal notes of sanctity and of the
invisible presence of the Spirit of Christ that Newman
turned. " External things are comparatively nothing "
wrote Newman in his letter to the Bishop of Oxford in
1841, " whatever be a religious body's relation to the
State—whatever its regimen—whatever its doctrines—
whatever its worship—if it has but the life of holiness
within it, this inward gift will, if I may so speak, take
care of itself. It will turn all accidents into good, it
will supply defects, and it will gain for itself, from above,
what is wanting. I desire to look at this first in all
persons and all communities. Where Almighty God
stirs the heart there his other gifts follow in time ;
sanctity is the great Note of the Church." [1]

Newman does not, of course, by this intend to deny
the dogmatic principle which he always regarded as
essential to Christianity. But he now believed that
the supreme criticism was to be found not in any
" paper theory," but in the supernatural life of the
Church—not " in the persuasive words of reason, but
in demonstration of the spirit and power, that faith
should stand not in the wisdom of Man, but in the
Power of God."

This is the belief that inspires Newman's last Anglican
sermons, which are the ripest fruits of his religious and
literary genius. No one can understand the Oxford
Movement who has not read and meditated these
great sermons, especially the series of Nov.-Dec., 1841,
on the inward notes of the Church and that of Nov.-

[1] Newman, *Via Media*, II, p. 408.

Dec., 1842, on "The Christian Empire." [1] for they express the spirit of the Movement in its purest form, disentangled from the ecclesiastical polemics and the controversial special pleading that disfigured its external history. They show us the movement not as a temporary reaction against the ecclesiastical legislation of the Reform Parliament, nor as an attempt to force the facts of history into the artificial mould of a paper theory, but in its essential character as a vindication of the supernatural character of Christianity—a supernatural order realized in the spiritual life of the individual Christian and in the corporate reality of a Divine Society.

The spiritual pilgrimage of the Oxford Movement was ended. It had led its followers through " darkness, and storm and the sound of words " to the vision of " Mount Sion, the City of the living God, the Heavenly Jerusalem, to the general assembly of the Church of the Firstborn which are written in heaven."

Note on the Later Developments of the Oxford Movement.

The new current which entered the Oxford Movement about 1839 has been somewhat neglected by the historians of the Movement, owing, on the one hand, to a dislike of its Romeward tendencies, and, on the other, to Newman's later alienation from Ward which led him to minimize the importance of his earlier relations with Ward and his friends. Actually this current had more in common with the original Tractarian tradition than is usually supposed, while it is

[1] In sermons on *Subjects of the Day*, Nos. xxi–xxiv and xiv–xvii.

also the source of many of the characteristic features of the later Anglo-Catholic development.

The position for which these younger men stood is stated in its most moderate form in the article in defence of Oakeley's views on the Reformation. "What is meant by Unprotestantizing the Church of England," in the *British Critic* for July, 1842 : "The forward movement," he writes, "aims only at an expansion and development of the present church system, *as it actually exists*. It is opposed to no principles of Church or State ; it has no precedent of ' tried and won't do ' stored up against it in the national history. . . . Far from being an alien or interloper, it sympathizes with the very central spirit and essence of the Church ; it identifies itself with this spirit, looks up to it as its source . . . it appeals to an ancient and still remaining life of the Church, only relieved from a modern language which has *overgrown* it, against a modern temper that has *invaded* it. Most cruel and unjust is the charge against followers of such a movement, that because they would relieve the Church and her divines from this outside and uncongenial coating . . . that they are therefore deserters and apostates from her. . . . They feel themselves connected with the Church by associations which stretch over her whole history. . . . Not in handing over one melancholy interval, which let in the puritan-Protestant spirit, to the historical appropriation of their opponents, do they at all forget what the Church and her divines have done since in the way of reaction from that spirit ; their pious and noble efforts in rescuing her from its most deadly grasp and its most serious development. A large and ample field on both sides of that epoch, they consider their own ground and that of the intrinsic Church. They claim Saxon saint and Norman prelate, templar and holy palmer, Christian knight and cloistered monk, and lower down the stream of time, their recollections pass on to grave Archbishop and Bishop, Royal Martyr and loyal Cavalier, and that faithful band who were confessors for the truth when ' a new king arose ' who disowned it. These and a thousand other associations bind them to their Church by an indissoluble tie, nor do they understand why it should follow that because they think that the Church *now* more than ever needs the help of her sons, that therefore they should abandon her. At all events, they are not going to do so ; they feel themselves solid and rightful members of her ; and they beg to offer it to the consideration of disinterested and impartial persons both in Church and State, which of two movements . . . is likely in the end to be most *revolutionary*, that which starts upon the basis and carries out the historical character of the Church, or that *which rejects the one and is rejected by the other*." This is the doctrine of Anglican continuity which has become the common teaching of moderate Anglo-Catholicism, and it is curious to find it put forward by the so-called Romanizing party in defence of their extremist tendencies.

VIII. *CONCLUSION*

SAMARIA

Oh, rail not at our kindred in the North,
  Albeit Samaria finds her likeness there ;
A self-form'd Priesthood, and the Church cast forth
  To the chill mountain air.

What, though their fathers sinned, and lost the grace
  Which seals the Holy Apostolic Line ?
Christ's love o'erflows the bounds His prophets trace
  In His reveal'd design.

Israel had seers ; to them the Word is nigh ;
  Shall not that Word run forth, and gladness give
To many a Shunammite, till in His eye
  The full Seven-thousand live ?

J. H. N.,

Off Sardinia.   *June* 17, 1833.

The limits of this essay do not permit me to deal with the later years of the Oxford Movement or the events that led up to the final cataclysm of 1845–46. To contemporaries, these events seemed to portend the collapse of the Oxford Movement and the ruin of its work. The consternation and uncertainty of the survivors is vividly described in the last chapter of Dean Church's book, as well as in the letters of Keble, Pusey, Marriott and others. For the loss of Newman left the party without a head, a collection of scattered groups and individuals with no common policy. The inner circle of the original Tractarians, such as Keble and Copeland and Isaac Williams, were too much affected by the shock to assume the leadership, and it was rather Manning and Robert Wilberforce who

attempted to rally the scattered forces of the movement
in the country, though they too were destined to follow
Newman in a few years. Meanwhile Pusey and
Marriott and Church kept the flag of Tractarian
principles flying at Oxford in the face of almost
insuperable difficulties. The Oxford Movement in
the strict sense was indeed at an end, but thanks to
Pusey, above all, its spirit survived to inspire the work
of the Anglo-Catholic revival in the country at large.

But this was by no means fully recognized by contemporary opinion. Pusey was at first regarded with
intense suspicion as the head of a Romanizing faction
which was secretly disloyal to the Church of England ;
and even his bishop, Samuel Wilberforce, could write
that Pusey's lack of humility and egotistic assumption
of leadership had led him into fearful errors.[1] The
moderate High Church party had experienced a
severe shock and did not wish to take any further
risks. They recognized the great services that Newman
nad done to the Church of England, but they felt that
at all costs a return must be made to the *Via Media*.
A remarkable example of this state of mind is to be
found in the final judgement passed on the work of
the Oxford Movement by one of its original members,
William Palmer of Worcester, at the close of his career.
He pays a generous tribute to Newman, whom he
regards as the author and sole leader of the movement
which resulted in the awakening of the English Church.
But, he continues, " Newman's teaching had been too
theoretical ; there was too much of speculation and
of controversy in it to fit it for permanency. But as it

[1] *Life of Wilberforce*, I, p. 311 (Letters of Nov. 9, 1845).

fell, a more practical and beneficial agency arose, which taking what was good and true in Newman's system, and accordant with the Church of England, placed these principles in a higher and nobler and more practical attitude. As it was said of Saul, ' He hath slain his thousands,' but David, ' his tens of thousands,' so it was in this case."

So far there is nothing surprising in this, and one might expect him to go on to a eulogy of Pusey's work. But Palmer's David is not Pusey, nor Keble nor even Church, it is *Samuel Wilberforce!* " Newman laid the foundations, but Wilberforce built up the temple. Wilberforce realized in the face of the world, high and low, the true ideal of a Christian episcopate in the Church of England—a model which was to furnish an example to all ages of the Church ; but never to be rivalled or approached again." [1]

This is very startling to the modern reader, but it is not quite so absurd as it seems at first sight. For the results of the Oxford Movement are to be seen in the development of the working compromise of the new Victorian *Via Media*, as well as in Puseyism and Ritualism and in the " Second Spring " of the Roman Catholic Church in England. The Church of England as it exists to-day owes more than is generally supposed to the work of Bishop Wilberforce, for it was he and the policy for which he stood which transformed the *Via Media* from a paper theory to a working system. It is an interesting example of development, though it

---

[1] Palmer, *Narrative of Events, etc.*, pp. 256–257. The appreciation of Newman's share in the Movement is more fully developed in his article on " The Oxford Movement " in the *Contemporary Review*, May, 1885.

does not satisfy the canons of Newman's theory, since it eliminates, or at least reduces to a minimum, the dogmatic principle on which the original *Via Media* had been founded. Still less would it have met with the approval of Hurrell Froude, for this development gave a new lease of life to Erastianism and restored the alliance of Church and State on a broader and more indefinite basis. It is true that this also owed a great deal to the Liberal Churchmen, the successors of Arnold and Whately, but it is doubtful if their views would have counted for much had it not been for the rise of this new middle party. Moreover, the change in the spirit of political Liberalism itself and its loss of the narrowly anticlerical tone that marked its earlier phase, may have been, in some measure, due to the influence of the Oxford Movement, as represented by such men as Mr. Gladstone.

Certainly it was not without its effect on the general tone of English culture in the 19th century. As Matthew Arnold wrote of Oxford in a well-known passage of *Culture and Anarchy*, " we have not won our political battles, we have not carried our main points, we have not stopped our adversaries' advance, we have not marched victoriously with the modern world ; but we have told silently upon the mind of the country, we have prepared currents of feeling which sap our adversaries' position when it seemed gained, we have kept up our communications with the future." " Who will estimate how much the currents of feeling created by Dr. Newman's movements, the keen desire for beauty and sweetness that it nourished, the deep aversion it manifested to the hardness and vulgarity of middle-class Liberalism, the strong light it turned on the hideous and grotesque illusions of middle-class Protestantism—who will estimate how much all these contributed to swell the tide of secret dissatisfaction which has mined the ground under the self-confident Liberalism of the last thirty years and has prepared the way for its sudden collapse and supersession ? "

But it is not in such dubious victories that the true significance of the Oxford Movement is to be found. It was not its mission to prepare the way for the Victorian compromise or to play the part of John the Baptist to Matthew Arnold's Messiah. If it stands for anything, it stands for religious truth, and if its religious ideals are false, then it is a spiritual *cul-de-sac* that has no relevance to living thought. No doubt the ecclesiastical controversies that marked the course of the movement are dead—so dead that it requires a considerable effort of imagination to realize that they ever were alive. Nevertheless the Tractarians were not a mere ecclesiastical party. They possessed, to a far greater extent than is usual in England, a common body of intellectual and spiritual principles which can be disentangled from the political and ecclesiastical circumstances of the time and which remains of vital importance for the religion of the modern world.

During the last century, European religion has been passing through the great crisis of its history. The Tractarians were the contemporaries not only of Arnold, and Hampden and Stanley, but of Strauss and Feuerbach and of Comte and Renan. The real religious issue before the age was not whether High Church or Low Church views should prevail in the

Church of England, but whether the Christian religion should preserve its spiritual identity, or whether it should be transformed by the spirit of the age and absorbed into the secularized culture of the modern world. In Catholic Europe this issue has assumed the form of a bitter struggle between the Church and the organized forces of anticlericalism, which have on the whole succeeded in de-Christianizing the State and public education without, however, affecting the spiritual autonomy and vitality of the Church itself. In Protestant Europe, on the other hand, the struggle has been an internal one which has had a profound effect on religious teaching and belief. There has always been an anti-supernatural tendency in Protestantism, which already shows itself clearly in the 18th century in such men as Bishop Hoadley, as well as, more directly, in Socinianism and Unitarianism. Protestantism was able to withstand this tendency only so long and in so far as it could appeal to an infallible organ of supernatural revelation. But with the development of the new biblical criticism in the 19th century, the objective and infallible character of Christian revelation gradually disappeared and a way was opened to the complete de-supernaturalization of Protestant Christianity. This tendency has been opposed by the anti-intellectual obscurantism of the Fundamentalists and by the illuminism of the more extreme Protestant sects, as well as, in recent years, by the attempt of the Barthians to restore the conception of the transcendence of divine revelation in the spirit of Calvin and the Reformers. It is, however, difficult to see how even the latter can maintain itself by a purely theological *tour de force* without any historical or institutional basis of authority, while Liberal Protestantism seems to possess no inherent principle capable of withstanding the growing pressure of secularized culture.

The Oxford Movement, however, brought a new element into the religious life of the 19th century. It stood above all for the preservation of the spiritual identity of Christianity, and represents an attempt to restore the Catholic conception of an objective supernatural order and the Catholic idea of divine authority within the boundaries of the Established Church of Protestant England. It was by Newman that these principles were most clearly realized, and through him that they received their full intellectual formulation, but in spite of the differences of character and mentality between the leaders of the Movement, Newman, Keble, Froude and Pusey were all in complete agreement on this fundamental issue. They all stood for Authority and Tradition against Liberalism, for Supernaturalism against Rationalism and Naturalism. The fundamental note of the Oxford Movement was its *anti-modernism*. It is true that they began on the political ground—in a protest against the secularization of the modern State and its claim to interfere with the rights of the Church. But almost at once the conflict became an internal one between the opposing forces in the Church of England—not, however, between High Church and Low Church, between Catholic and Evangelical, but between religious Traditionalism and religious Liberalism. In fact, the first great battle that the Tractarians fought—that against Dr. Hampden—

was one in which they had the support of the Evangelicals.

Now Dr. Hampden held—or was supposed to have held—the characteristically Modernist view of dogma. A theological dogma was not the infallible definition of a revealed truth, it was the expression of the thought of a particular age, and reflected the passing fashions of the dominant philosophy. But philosophy is not religion, and consequently the Christian thinker has every right to exercise his powers of criticism in order to disentangle the kernel of religious truth from the mask of its temporary theological formulation. The modern age was not bound to the creeds of the past. It could form its own intellectual statement of Christianity out of the resources of its richer knowledge and its wider spiritual sympathies.

It is obvious that this is nothing more nor less than Modernism in the full theological sense, although it was not as yet applied to the Biblical text or the Gospel narrative. But the essence of Modernism is to be found not in historical criticism, but in the anti-dogmatic principle—in other words, it is identical with what Newman described as Liberalism. In the case of a man like von Hügel, we feel at once that he was no true Modernist however much he may have shared the views of the Modernists in critical matters, because he whole-heartedly accepted the dogmatic principle of Catholicism—the existence of a divine Truth and a divine Authority to which the human mind and will must conform themselves. To the true Modernist, man is the measure of all things and the spirit of the age is the spirit of God. To say that a belief or a moral law is "unmodern" is to condemn it, for in the eyes of the Modernist there are no eternal truths and no divine law other than the law of change.

Now the historical significance of the Oxford Movement is to be found, above all, in its recognition of the vital importance of this issue and in its acceptance of the Liberal challenge. It stood *pro causa Dei* against the apostasy of the modern world. The contemporary Catholic revival on the Continent was, no doubt, fighting the same enemy as the Oxford Movement, but it was fighting it as an external enemy ; whereas for the Tractarians the enemy was already within the camp, seventy years before the same thing occurred within the Catholic Church.

The fact that the leaders of the Movement, Keble and Pusey and the rest, could retain their confidence in Newman and their devotion to him after his conversion was due to their belief that they were still engaged in a common warfare with a common enemy. However profound were the differences which kept them apart from the Catholic Church, they could not condemn it for the same reasons as the average educated Englishman did—as the enemy of civilization and progress— for there they stood on precisely the same ground. When in the '60's Pius IX's publication of the *Syllabus of Modern Errors* aroused a howl of execration from Protestant and Liberal Europe, Oakeley could say with perfect truth that the teaching of Pius IX was the same teaching that he had heard on the lips of Keble and Hurrell Froude. The Pope's famous condemnation of the proposition " that the Church can and ought to reconcile itself with Liberalism, Progress and Modern Civilization " is precisely the view of the leaders of the Oxford Movement, and it might well serve as a motto for the *Remains* of Hurrell Froude and *Lyra Apostolica*, Newman's sermon on the Spirit of the Age, and Keble's sermon on National Apostasy.

To the Liberal, the truth of this proposition seems so obvious that to condemn it is an act of blasphemous folly, and consequently this sentence in the *Syllabus* has always shocked the Liberal mind in the same way as the denial of God or of the immortality of the human soul shocks the Christian. To the Tractarians, on the other hand, it was self-evident that the Church could not reconcile itself with the anti-dogmatic and anti-authoritarian principle which is the essence of Liberalism, while Progress, which is simply the natural process of cultural change, needs no inherent claim to the allegiance of a Christian. And in the same way it was impossible for them to regard modern civilization as an absolute good, so long as it represented the apostasy of the modern world and the revolt of Christendom against the Christian tradition.

This was the main issue of the Oxford Movement, and all its measures of ecclesiastical and liturgical reform were subordinated to this central preoccupation. If Keble or Pusey returned to see the results of their work to-day, they would not judge it by the changes that it has produced in ecclesiastical ceremonial. They would not pay great attention to the increase in the use of vestments and incense and Gregorian chant. They would ask whether there was more supernatural faith in the Church of England to-day than there was a century ago—whether there was a stronger hold on dogma and a more objective view of spiritual truth. And it would not be easy to answer in the affirmative since the success of the Anglo-Catholic movement in all that concerns the externals of worship has been accompanied by a no less remarkable advance of Liberalism and Modernism in matters of faith. But what would most alarm and scandalize the spirits of Keble and Pusey is that these two tendencies are no longer sharply defined and mutually hostile movements. They co-exist with one another in the very bosom of the Anglo-Catholic party itself.

It is easy to find men who accept all the externals of Catholic worship but who at the same time sit loose not to the thirty-nine articles but to the three creeds. As the Dean of Exeter has recently written in an Anglo-Catholic periodical : " Anglo - Catholic theologians have been and are among the most distinguished and sometimes the most drastic of Biblical critics ; and the Modernism of Tyrrell and Loisy, driven underground in the Roman Church, has found a congenial home in Anglo-Catholic theology. The reactionary politics of the Oxford Movement which were against the modest attempts to diffuse ' useful knowledge ' against reform and not intolerant of slavery, have given place to politics of the left and an affinity has been discovered between the Catholic Faith and Socialism, or even Communism. There is, it appears, no incompatibility between the Mass and the red flag." [1] Hence Dr. Matthews finds the real achievement of the Oxford Movement in the formation of a new type of Free

[1] *The Green Quarterly.* 1933, p. 71.

Catholicism in which the tradition of the Church is " thought of, not as an unchanging deposit, but as the creative spirit manifested through the developing experiences of the worshipping community," and which interprets the sacramental idea " not in a legalistic manner but with the freedom of poetry." [1]

The Dean is not himself an Anglo-Catholic, but there is a good deal in modern Anglo-Catholic literature which justifies his statements. Even the centenary of the Oxford Movement has been made the occasion of a justification of the ideals of a religious Liberalism which would have been supremely distasteful to the leaders of the Movement themselves. Yet the most recent Anglo-Catholic biography of John Keble even attempts to make that arch-traditionalist and arch-conservative the patron of Anglo-Catholic Modernism. It claims that Keble points the way towards a possible alternative to traditional Catholicism, to a Liberal Catholicism which will be humanitarian and individualistic instead of authoritarian and traditionalist and which will freely co-operate with other forms of religion in a common religious message.[2]

Whatever we may think of this ideal, there can be no question as to what John Keble would have thought of it. In his eyes it was impossible for Catholicism to " make contact with the evolution of the modern mind " by a surrender of the dogmatic principle, and if he had thought that " the genius of the Church of England " demanded such a surrender, he would have thought it a duty to surrender his membership of an

[1] *Ibid.*, p. 75.
[2] *John Keble*, by Kenneth Ingram (1933).

apostate Church. In fact, these new tendencies are the very tendencies towards " nominalism " and modernism which he denounced so unsparingly in his famous sermon on Tradition, which reflects his fundamental position much more completely than his other famous sermon on National Apostasy. And nothing perhaps shows the change in the spirit of Anglo-Catholicism more than the extent to which it has receded from that high-watermark of Anglican dogmatic orthodoxy.

This change in the spirit of Anglo-Catholicism is also shown in its attitude to Rome—not that the Tractarians were lacking in hostility to Roman doctrine, but because their hostility rested on totally different grounds. To the Tractarians the great rock of offence was the worship of the saints and their images which they, like the Reformers, regarded as essentially idolatrous. The modern Anglo-Catholics, on the other hand, are scandalized at the very points on which Rome and the Tractarians are at one—its traditionalism and authoritarianism, its hostility to Liberalism and its belief in the infallibility of the Bible. For example, in a recent article Mr. Kenneth Ingram quotes the very passage from the *Syllabus* of Pius IX which I have already referred to as embodying the essential principle of the Oxford Movement, whereas he uses it as a self-evident proof that Rome is always wrong.[1]

At first sight this *volte face* seems inexplicable. When the Liberal movement was sweeping everything before it, and when it had on its side the weight of popular opinion and the most brilliant minds of the

[1] *The Green Quarterly*, 1933, p. 83.

age, the founders of Anglo-Catholicism stood out against it and anathematized it. To-day, when Liberalism is a spent force, when hardly anyone believes in Progress, and when modern civilization seems self-dedicated to destruction, we find the heirs of the Oxford Movement (or some of them at least) surrendering their post to an enemy that is in full retreat. But the ultimate cause of this contradiction is to be found in the later history of the Oxford Movement itself. No movement can live by Tradition alone, even if it be the tradition of Keble and Pusey. It needs positive intellectual principles. But the men who gave the Movement its intellectual character were just those who left it for Rome. Keble and Pusey were great moral forces, but they were not thinkers. By their personal influence they saved the Anglo-Catholic tradition for the Church of England. But they were unable to supply the place of Newman. His departure left an intellectual void which was left unfilled or filled with improvised and heterogeneous material. This has remained the weak spot in the later development of the Movement, and it explains the intrusion of an intellectual element that is entirely incongruous with its original spirit. Nevertheless, it is difficult to see how such an element can be permanently incorporated with the Anglo-Catholic tradition. One element must ultimately expel the other. Either the existence of the Tractarian tradition will provide the basis for a return to Catholic intellectual principles, or the Movement will become so penetrated by modernist of them that it will no longer possess any fundamental opposition to Liberal Protestantism and will ultimately tend to coalesce with it in the amorphous unity of a creedless undenominationalism.

But if it does so, it will be only for a moment. The time for such compromises is over. They might have been successful in the 19th century, when the victories of Liberalism and material progress combined to give men the illusion that all was for the best in the best of all possible civilizations, and that the traditional opposition between the Church and the World had lost its meaning.

But it is no longer so to-day when

> the dark comes on apace
> When none can work for fear,
> And Liberty in every Land lies slain
> And the Two Tyrannies unchallenged reign
> And heavy prophecies, suspended long
> At supplication of the righteous few
> And so discredited, to fulfilment throng, . . .

The Tractarians were not deceived by these illusions. They read the signs of the times better than the men who professed to be in sympathy with the spirit of the age. They knew where the world was going and they would not have been surprised by the atheism of modern Russia or the materialism of modern mass-civilization. They believed that Christianity was once more faced with the prospect of persecution and that it must be prepared for a long struggle against the powers of the world.

" Is there not at this very time," asked the *Tracts for the Times*, " a special effort made all over the world . . . but most visibly and formidably in its most civilized and powerful parts, an effort to do without Religion ? . . . An attempt to make numbers and not the Truth the ground of maintaining, or not maintaining, this or that creed, as if we had any reason whatever in Scripture for thinking that the many will be in the right, and the few in the wrong? An attempt to deprive the Bible of its one meaning to the exclusion of others, to make people think that it may have an hundred meanings all equally good, or in other words that it has no meaning at all, is a dead letter and may be put aside? An attempt to supersede Religion altogether as far as it is external or objective, as far as it is displayed in ordinances, or can be expressed by written words,—to confine it to our inward feelings, and thus, considering, how variable, how evanescent our feelings are, an attempt in fact to destroy Religion?

" Surely there is at this day a confederacy of evil, marshalling its hosts from all parts of the world, organizing itself, taking its measures, enclosing the Church of Christ as in a net, and preparing the way for a general Apostasy from it. . . .

" Shall we Christians allow ourselves to have lot or part in this matter? Shall we even with our little finger help on the Mystery of Iniquity which is travailing for birth and convulsing the earth with its pangs? ' O my soul come not thou into their secret; unto their assembly, mine honour, be not thou united.' What fellowship hath righteousness with unrighteousness? and what communion hath light with darkness? Wherefore come out from among them, and be ye separate ' . . . lest you be workers together with God's enemies, and be opening the way for the Man of sin, the son of perdition.' " [1]

The apocalyptic spirit which finds its clearest

[1] Tract 85.

expression in this passage underlies all the teaching of
the early Tractarians, and of all the features of the
Movement it is probably the one that it is hardest for
the modern reader to understand or to sympathize
with. Nevertheless, it is one of the authentic notes of
historic Christianity, and, if we ignore it, we shall find
it impossible to understand not only the spirit of the
Oxford Movement but the spirit of the New Testament
itself.